# HIT!

## SARAH COATES

# CONTENTS

# INTRODUCTION

*LET'S MAKE SOME BAD DECISIONS. THEY WILL BE KICK-ASS, TOTALLY DELICIOUS AND SOMETIMES UNEXPECTED BAD DECISIONS – AND WE'LL BE MAKING THEM ALL IN THE KITCHEN. I'M TALKING ABOUT PUTTING CAKE IN MILKSHAKES, EATING LUSCIOUS PANCAKES FOR BREAKFAST AND HAND-DIPPING YOUR OWN CHOCOLATE-COATED ICE CREAM CONES. THE GOOD NEWS IS THAT THERE'S NOTHING SO TERRIBLE HERE THAT CAN'T BE UNDONE WITH A LITTLE JUDICIOUS DIETING AND HITTING THE PAVEMENT – SO IT'S NOT LIKE PIERCING YOUR NIPPLE OR TATTOOING 'WINONA FOREVER' ON YOUR ARM!*

Cooking from a recipe is a strange form of hanging out. If you're lucky, over time you get to know the person who wrote the recipe and really grow to like them because they keep giving you good food. Whether that person is physically in the kitchen with you or not doesn't really matter. A lot of the time they probably won't be. I've gotten to know so many people through their books, blogs or YouTube channels. Either way, they always feel like friends because they're trying to help me out.

Sometimes the person is a maternal influence, like Martha Stewart, who is bossy but always right. Sometimes it's an impossibly chic and awesome older woman, who you just wish you were as cool as, like Nigella Lawson. And sometimes they feel like an older sister or a sassy friend, like Joy the Baker, Gizzi Erskine or Jemma Wilson – who are just like me but with a whole arsenal of amazing tricks up their sleeves, which I'm dying to learn.

Think of me as your cheeky younger sister. I'm not a responsible older sibling who's going to teach you how to apply lip-liner correctly, or explain why you should eat kale salad (why?). I'm still working out those adult skills myself (you should see me try and apply lip-liner). What I have got worked out, though, is the short-cut route to the best, sexiest and tastiest sweet things for those days when it is time to CUT LOOSE and enjoy yourself.

If you and I were going to be in a water bomb fight, I would fill our balloons with jelly instead of water, to give us the edge over the competition. That's the same attitude that I have brought to this book. I have used every dirty trick in my arsenal to lead you to victory when it comes to tearing it up in the kitchen. I have tested, re-tested and mad scientist-ed this whole book to get down to the MOST delicious, MOST ridiculous, MOST fun bunch of Sugar Hit goodness I could come up with.

As a blogger who jumped the hell out of the rat race at the very first opportunity, I am a HUGE believer in the 'life's too short' mentality. I know that's hardly an original thought, but I feel like it's never more important than when you're looking at a book full of sweet snacks and desserts. If you want to bake something, I am more than happy to be that little imp on your shoulder screaming 'YES YOU SHOULD!', because I totally think that life is for the living and cake is for the eating. Pancakes forever, dieting never!

So what can you expect to find in here? I've broken it down into six chapters. The first is Breakfast & Brunch. As American comic TV character Ron Swanson said, 'There has never been a sadness that can't be cured by breakfast foods'. So that was a no-brainer.

From there I moved on to the Coffee Break chapter, because that's how my mind works – as soon as breakfast is over, I'm already thinking about my mid-morning snack-attack.

In the Healthy Junk chapter, you'll find something for every day of the year. Something for your vegan friend, your gluten-free niece and for those days when you want to eat rice pudding but also feel healthy and full of life.

From there, things take a devious turn in the Midnight Snacks chapter. I'm so excited about that chapter. I'm not going to say anything more about it. Just wait till you get there.

Party Time is all about layer cakes, giant pies and show-stopping desserts. These are the things to pull out for a graduation, engagement or twenty-first birthday – they are recipes that really make eyes light up. Stick a bunch of sparklers in the top of any one of these and make someone's day.

And, finally, because I am absolutely, hopelessly in love with the festive season, the last chapter is Happy Holidays. It's full of all the things that I want to make and eat while staring at twinkling lights and singing Christmas carols loudly and off-key.

I hope you find something in here that makes you feel like you just have to make it straight away. And I hope you share it with a friend or a loved one. And I hope it makes you and them as happy as all these recipes have made me. Because life is short, and butter is the best!

Let's do this!

# KITCHEN NOTES

### BUTTER

My rebellious streak refuses to bow to the conventional wisdom that unsalted butter should be used in baking. I like salted butter – it's what I put on my toast, so that's what I use. If you're using unsalted, no dramas, just be generous with any additional salt!

### CHOCOLATE AND COCOA

When it comes to chocolate it definitely pays to shop for quality. This is one of those instances where you definitely get what you pay for. Always go for at least 70 per cent cocoa solids in dark chocolate, and at least 35–40 per cent in milk chocolate and shop around to find your favourite brand. For unsweetened (Dutch) cocoa powder, I think the darker the better. I tend to go for an organic brand, which is almost black and full of flavour.

### COCONUT OIL

The two kinds of coconut oil you're likely to see at the shops are virgin and refined. There's a lot of debate about the relative health merits of each. I use coconut oil, not for health reasons, but because it solidifies at cold room temperature and has a great taste. Virgin coconut oil tastes strongly of coconut, while refined oil has a much more subtle, nutty flavour. Either one will work for the recipes in this book.

### DEEP-FRYING

... is the funnest! But it's also, obviously, not something that you want to muck around with. My tips for deep-frying are as follows:

*   Pick a heavy, sturdy pan to deep-fry in
*   Use an oil with a high smoke-point, such as canola or grapeseed
*   Put your pan on a burner at the back of the stove, not the front
*   Make sure any handles aren't hanging over the side of the work surface
*   Invest in a thermometer to measure the temperature of the oil
*   Never fill your pan more than a third full of oil
*   Leave the oil to cool completely before disposing of it
*   Use common sense!

## EGGS

All eggs are large, free-range and organic in my kitchen. I'm happy to pay a little more if it means that one less chicken has to live a horrible battery-cage existence. Organic eggs taste fantastic and they're better for you, but any large eggs will do.

## FLOUR

The two main types of flour used in this book are plain (all-purpose) flour and strong flour (sometimes called bread flour). Strong flour has a little extra protein, making it better suited to bread baking. I recommend that you use strong flour, where it's mentioned, for the best results.

## LINING A TIN WITH ACETATE

Acetate is a food-safe plastic, which you can use to line a cake tin when you want a really tall finish, or are working with liquid fillings that need time to set. You can buy it from specialty cake stores. Simply set up your springform tin as usual, and then line the plastic inside the tin, using masking tape on the outside to hold it in place. You may need to use two pieces to get a high enough rim. True confession – I have been known to use clear A4 pieces of stationery plastic in a pinch.

## SALTED CARAMEL

I know it's hardly original, but this stuff is just so good, and so useful in the kitchen. This is my fail-safe recipe. The sugar is, of course, boiling hot, so give it your full attention. Don't touch it and be very careful. This recipe makes 400 ml (13½ fl oz).

230 G (8 OZ/1 CUP) CASTER (SUPERFINE) SUGAR
125 ML (4 FL OZ/½ CUP) POURING (SINGLE/LIGHT) CREAM (35% FAT)
125 G (4½ OZ) BUTTER, CHOPPED
1 TEASPOON SEA SALT FLAKES

Put the sugar in a deep heavy-based saucepan over medium heat, along with 60 ml (2 fl oz/¼ cup) water. Cook, without stirring, until the sugar melts and the mixture begins to bubble. If the sugar is melting unevenly, you can tilt and swirl the pan gently, but do not stir. Once the mixture begins to bubble, continue cooking for 5–8 minutes until the sugar darkens to an amber colour – you might see some wisps of smoke from the pan, but that's normal.

Remove the pan from the heat and carefully pour in the cream. It will bubble up furiously, but just leave it to settle. Then add the butter, put the pan back over low heat and cook, stirring, until everything melts and combines into a gorgeous caramel. Stir in the salt.

## SUGAR

In almost all of my baking I use caster (superfine) sugar. It is exactly the same as regular white granulated sugar, just a little finer. I find that it dissolves more readily and evenly in a batter or dough, making it ideal for baking. But in most cases, regular granulated sugar would be a fine substitute.

## VANILLA BEAN PASTE

I have a major crush on this stuff. Ground vanilla beans suspended in a thick syrup is a much more aromatic way of getting vanilla into your food than using an extract or essence. It's pretty expensive, but less so than buying beans constantly. Feel free to substitute good-quality natural vanilla extract.

# BREAKFAST & BRUNCH

As far as I'm concerned, there's no such thing as a bad breakfast. No matter what you put into your body first thing in the morning, there is a mood and excitement to breakfast that simply cannot be ignored. I love that I can take on a whole new persona every morning. Will I have an edgy cup of black coffee, snatched on a rushed commute and dripping with Gallic attitude? A towering, generous stack of pancakes, swimming in maple syrup and enjoyed while wrapped in a lumberjack flannel? Or an energetic bowl of lush yoghurt and fresh fruit, eaten after a walk on the beach? Whatever I end up having, it lets me set the tone for the day.

Breakfast and brunch also happen to be great gateways to cooking. Even the most kitchen-challenged person can manage to get up and make themselves a piece of toast in the morning. And anyone who knows how to pour a bowl of cereal can stir together a batch of Best bircher muesli (page 12). From there, it's a hop, skip and a jump to a simple batch of Poppy seed French toast with whipped ricotta (page 14) or a Vanilla bean Dutch baby with cherry-bourbon compote (page 28). Before you know it, you're sitting down to a brunch spread of epic proportions!

There's nothing I love more than having people over for brunch. Can we have more brunch gatherings as a group, please? Brunch has so much going for it. First, everyone loves breakfast foods. Second, you get to skip the over-crowded cafés and avoid depressing hipster service. Finally, and most importantly, it's such an easy way to entertain. Most things can either be prepared the night before or easily kept warm in a low oven. And, as long as there's plenty of coffee, stacks of toast and butter, and maybe a buck's fizz or two, everyone will be having a great time anyway. The only thing I can't help you with at breakfast is getting out of bed at a reasonable hour. I'm terrible at it.

# BEST BIRCHER MUESLI

*Have you heard of 'Columbusing'? It's a term used to describe the phenomenon of one person or a group of people 'discovering' something, which another group of people have known about for a really long time. Like, for example, when Christopher Columbus 'discovered' America, even though Native Americans had been living there for thousands of years, and a Viking expedition had settled there years before. Whatever the thing is, the 'discoverers' usually re-brand it with a new name and then start walking around acting like they invented it. I feel this is what happened recently with the trend for 'overnight oats'. That's the Columbus name for bircher muesli. Bircher. Muesli. Invented by Dr Bircher-Benner of Switzerland around 1900. It's so good that I'm not surprised people would try and claim it as their own. But I'm such an Alp-o-phile that I love the idea of eating a Swiss mountain breakfast, and I fully embrace the cool history of this dish. This is my favourite version, heavy on the apples, just like the original. Great with a breath of fresh Alpine air.*

100 G (3½ OZ/1 CUP) WHOLE ROLLED (PORRIDGE) OATS
310 ML (10½ FL OZ/1¼ CUPS) APPLE JUICE
45 G (1½ OZ/¼ CUP) DATES, SLICED
45 G (1½ OZ/¼ CUP) DRIED APRICOTS, SLICED
45 G (1½ OZ/¼ CUP) DRIED CRANBERRIES (CRAISINS)
2 SMALL GRANNY SMITH APPLES, GRATED
375 G (13 OZ/1½ CUPS) GREEK-STYLE YOGHURT
2 TABLESPOONS HONEY
FLAKED ALMONDS AND/OR CHOPPED HAZELNUTS, TO SERVE

Put the oats, juice, dried fruits and apple in a large bowl. Stir to combine then cover with plastic wrap and place in the refrigerator overnight.

To serve, place the yoghurt in a small bowl and ripple through the honey.

Divide the muesli and honeyed yoghurt between four small bowls, scatter over the nuts and serve.

Serves 4

# POPPY SEED FRENCH TOAST WITH WHIPPED RICOTTA

*I FIRST SAW THE ADDITION OF POPPY SEEDS TO FRENCH TOAST IN DAVID LOFTUS'S BRILLIANT BOOK AROUND THE WORLD IN 80 DISHES. I'M A HUGE FAN OF MR LOFTUS, BOTH AS AN AUTHOR (HIS BOOK MIRRORS JULES VERNE'S AROUND THE WORLD IN 80 DAYS THROUGH FOOD – GENIUS) AND AS A PHOTOGRAPHER (HE WORKS WITH JAMIE OLIVER, RACHEL KHOO AND A BUNDLE OF OTHERS). AFTER TRYING HIS RECIPE OUT, I NOW TOTALLY ADMIRE HIM AS A COOK, TOO. THIS IS MY TWEAKED VERSION, COMPLETE WITH CREAMY WHIPPED RICOTTA AND A PILE OF RASPBERRIES.*

## POPPY SEED FRENCH TOAST
3 EGGS
125 ML (4 FL OZ/$\frac{1}{2}$ CUP) MILK
1 TABLESPOON HONEY
1 TABLESPOON POPPY SEEDS
4 SLICES BRIOCHE (PREFERABLY DAY-OLD), OR OTHER STALE BREAD
BUTTER FOR FRYING

## WHIPPED RICOTTA
250 G (9 OZ/1 CUP) FRESH RICOTTA
$1\frac{1}{2}$ TABLESPOONS CASTER (SUPERFINE) SUGAR
1 TEASPOON VANILLA BEAN PASTE

## TO SERVE
FRESH RASPBERRIES
MAPLE SYRUP

To make the French toast, in a bowl, whisk together the eggs, milk, honey and poppy seeds.

Put the slices of brioche in a shallow dish and pour over the egg mixture. Leave to soak, turning occasionally, until almost all of the egg mixture is absorbed, about 10 minutes.

Meanwhile, to make the whipped ricotta, place all the ingredients in a food processor or blender and process the mixture until the ricotta goes from a grainy, crumbly texture to silky smooth. Scrape the mixture into a serving bowl.

Add about 20 g (¾ oz) butter to a large frying pan over medium–low heat. Once the butter is melted, add the pieces of soaked brioche, and cook slowly for about 2 minutes on each side or until golden brown and cooked through. Serve warm with the whipped ricotta, fresh raspberries and a drizzle of maple syrup.

Serves 2

# RICOTTA, BLUEBERRY AND BUTTERMILK PANCAKES

*IF YOU MAKE ABSOLUTELY NOTHING ELSE IN THIS BOOK, PLEASE MAKE THESE PANCAKES. THEY ARE BEAUTIFULLY FLUFFY WITH CUSTARDY, MILKY RICOTTA AND BURSTING BLUEBERRIES THROUGHOUT. DRIZZLED WITH MAPLE SYRUP AND TOPPED WITH SOME SALTED BUTTER … THEY'RE THE BEST. JUST MAKE THEM!*

150 G (5½ OZ/1 CUP) PLAIN (ALL-PURPOSE) FLOUR
1 TEASPOON BAKING POWDER
55 G (2 OZ/¼ CUP) CASTER (SUPERFINE) SUGAR
190 ML (6½ FL OZ/¾ CUP) BUTTERMILK
2 EGGS, SEPARATED
PINCH OF SALT
150 G (5½ OZ) FRESH RICOTTA
115 G (4 OZ/¾ CUP) FRESH BLUEBERRIES

Put the flour, baking powder and sugar in a bowl and stir together with a spatula. Add the buttermilk and stir until just combined – don't worry about lumps.

Put the egg yolks in with the flour mixture and stir the yolks into the batter.

In a separate bowl, whisk the egg whites and salt to stiff peaks.

Crumble the ricotta into the batter bowl, then dump all of the whisked whites on top of that. Fold the whites and ricotta into the batter until there are no more streaks of egg white.

Heat a non-stick frying pan over medium–low heat. Ladle about 2 tablespoons of batter into the pan and scatter over a few blueberries. Cook for 1½ minutes, then flip and cook for a further minute. Repeat with the remaining batter until all the pancakes are cooked, then serve.

Serves 2–3

# SUPA-THICK YOGHURT AND BERRIES

250 G (9 OZ/1 CUP) GREEK-STYLE YOGHURT
125 G (4½ OZ/½ CUP) CRÈME FRAÎCHE
1 TABLESPOON CASTER (SUPERFINE) SUGAR, OR TO TASTE

*BERRIES*
250 G (9 OZ/1²/₃ CUPS) STRAWBERRIES
125 G (4½ OZ/1 CUP) BLACKBERRIES
125 G (4½ OZ/1 CUP) RASPBERRIES
1 TEASPOON ROSEWATER
1-2 TEASPOONS CASTER (SUPERFINE) SUGAR, OR TO TASTE

The night before, stir together the yoghurt, crème fraîche and sugar. Set a sieve over a bowl and line the sieve with muslin (cheesecloth) or several layers of paper towel. Pour the yoghurt mixture into the lined sieve, cover with plastic wrap and leave in the refrigerator overnight.

The next morning, spread the yoghurt on a plate or dollop into a bowl.

Wash all the berries and halve the strawberries. Toss all of the berries with the rosewater and sugar. (It is best if you can leave them to macerate for a little while – even 10 minutes.) Spoon them over the yoghurt and dig in!

Serves 2

# BLUEBERRY AND ALMOND MORNING BUNS

THESE BUNS ARE THE CULMINATION OF SO MANY AWESOME THINGS. THE FLAKY, BUTTERY DOUGH IS REMINISCENT OF A CROISSANT. THE LAYERS OF CARAMELISED SUGAR BORROW FROM THE FAMOUS BRETON CAKE, KOUIGN AMANN, AND THE INSPIRATION FOR THESE 'MORNING BUNS' COMES FROM THE SAN FRANCISCO BAKERY, TARTINE. SCATTERED WITH BLUEBERRIES AND FLAKED ALMONDS AND BAKED IN A MUFFIN TIN, THE BUNS ARE CHEWY AND CRISP AND ARE AT THEIR BEST STRAIGHT OUT OF THE OVEN, SERVED WITH A 'LONDON FOG' (SEE TIP OPPOSITE).

300 G (10½ OZ/2 CUPS) PLAIN (ALL-PURPOSE) FLOUR
1 TEASPOON DRY ACTIVE YEAST
125 ML (4 FL OZ/½ CUP) WARM WATER
1 EGG
200 G (7 OZ) BUTTER
1 VANILLA BEAN
115 G (4 OZ/½ CUP) CASTER (SUPERFINE) SUGAR
100 G (3½ OZ/⅔ CUP) FRESH OR FROZEN BLUEBERRIES
30 G (1 OZ/⅓ CUP) FLAKED ALMONDS

In a medium mixing bowl (or the bowl of a stand mixer, with the dough hook attached) combine the flour, yeast, warm water and egg. Mix the ingredients together until they form a dough.

Transfer the dough to a floured work surface and knead for about 10 minutes (or knead for 5 minutes using a stand mixer) until the dough is smooth and elastic. Cover with plastic wrap and leave in a warm place for an hour or until doubled in size.

Once the dough has risen, lightly flour a work surface and roll into a 30 x 40 cm (12 x 16 in) rectangle with the short side facing you.

Slice the butter thinly and place it in the middle half of the dough, leaving a quarter of the dough exposed at the top and bottom. Fold the top and bottom pieces of dough over the butter, so they meet in the middle and the butter is covered. Then, fold the right- and left-hand edges of the dough into the middle. Fold the whole thing in half, so the seam is on the left. Press the dough firmly down to seal it and roll it back out to 30 x 40 cm (12 x 16 in). Repeat the same folding process, then wrap tightly in plastic wrap and place in the refrigerator for 2 hours or overnight

When you're ready to bake, preheat the oven to 200°C (400°F).

Split the vanilla bean, scrape out the seeds and rub them into the sugar.

Dust a work surface with about a quarter of the sugar. Take the dough out of the refrigerator and dust the top of it with another quarter of the sugar. Roll the dough out into a 30 x 40 cm (12 x 16 in) rectangle (using more sugar to dust if necessary). Spread any remaining sugar over the surface of the dough before scattering over the blueberries and almonds.

Roll the dough up tightly like a Swiss (jelly) roll and slice into 9 rounds. Put the rounds in a non-stick 12-hole muffin tin and set aside to rise for 15 minutes. Bake for 30 minutes, or until they are a deep golden brown. Leave to cool for a minute in the tin, before carefully turning out onto a wire rack to cool completely. Serve.

*Makes 9*

**TIP** Ever heard of a London Fog? It's an Earl Grey tea latte, sweetened with a shot of vanilla. To make a cheat's version, put a mugful of milk with a little vanilla bean paste (or natural vanilla extract), some sugar and an Earl Grey tea bag in a small saucepan over medium-low heat. Cook until tiny bubbles begin to appear at the edge of the pan. Turn off the heat, steep for a minute, remove the tea bag and whisk madly to create a bit of froth.

*THE PURSUIT OF A REALLY GOOD CINNAMON BUN HAS TAKEN ME TO THE KITCHEN AND KEPT ME THERE. TO ME, THESE LITTLE BUNS REPRESENT THE KIND OF COSY, FUN-FILLED, CROWDED LIFE THAT I'M ALWAYS CHASING — AND THE BEST THING IS THAT THEY OFTEN DELIVER IT. IF THERE'S ONE SURE-FIRE WAY TO LURE PEOPLE INTO THE KITCHEN, IT'S TO BAKE A GIANT CINNAMON BUN. THE BALANCE OF SPICE TO SUGAR TO BEAUTIFULLY LIGHT AND BUTTERY DOUGH IS ABSOLUTELY CRUCIAL. THIS BONKERS VERSION IS THE ULTIMATE.*

25 G (1 OZ) BUTTER, MELTED
115 G (4 OZ/½ CUP, FIRMLY PACKED) BROWN SUGAR
1 TABLESPOON GROUND CINNAMON
30 G (1 OZ/¼ CUP) CHOPPED PECANS, PLUS EXTRA, TO SERVE

*DOUGH*
75 G (2¾ OZ) BUTTER
190 ML (6½ FL OZ/¾ CUP) MILK
450 G (1 LB/3 CUPS) STRONG FLOUR
55 G (2 OZ/¼ CUP) CASTER (SUPERFINE) SUGAR
1½ TEASPOONS DRY ACTIVE YEAST
PINCH OF SALT
1 EGG, BEATEN

*ICING*
160 G (5½ OZ/⅔ CUP) CREAM CHEESE, AT ROOM TEMPERATURE
85 G (3 OZ/⅔ CUPS) ICING (CONFECTIONERS') SUGAR
1 TEASPOON VANILLA BEAN PASTE

To make the dough, melt the butter in a small saucepan over low heat, add the milk, then remove from the heat and set aside to cool slightly. Put the remaining dough ingredients and the slightly cooled milk and butter mixture in a large bowl and stir to bring the mixture together. On a floured work surface (or using a stand mixer), knead until a smooth, elastic and ever-so-slightly tacky dough forms. Put the dough back in the bowl and cover with plastic wrap. Leave in a warm place to rise for 30–45 minutes, or until doubled in size.

While the dough is rising, grease and line a 23 cm (9 in) round springform cake tin. When the dough has risen, punch it down and turn it out onto a lightly floured work surface again. Roll the dough out into a 30 cm (12 in) square. Spread the melted butter over the dough and sprinkle over the brown sugar, cinnamon and pecans. Slice the dough lengthways into 6 equal strips. Roll the first strip up in a spiral, just like a regular cinnamon bun. Roll the next strip around the first one, and then one more strip after that. Now plonk this giant bun in your greased tin, and drape and wrap the remaining strips of dough around it. You should end up with a very ramshackle giant cinnamon roll. Cover the tin with plastic wrap and set aside for about 45 minutes to rise.

Preheat the oven to 180°C (350°F). When the bun has risen, remove the plastic wrap and bake for 35–45 minutes, or until golden, risen and cooked through. Remove the bun from the tin and leave to cool until just warm.

For the icing, beat together all the ingredients, slather the mixture over the top of the bun, scatter over the extra pecans and tear into it.

Serves 8–10

# SKILLET CORNBREAD WITH BURNT HONEY BUTTER

*EVERYBODY WANTS TO BE SOUTHERN, RIGHT? AND I MEAN FROM THE SOUTHERN STATES OF THE USA — TO SPEAK WITH A DRAWL, SAY 'YA'LL' AND HAVE THE GENETIC ABILITY TO MAKE EXCELLENT FRIED CHICKEN. THAT CANNOT JUST BE ME. BUT SADLY I'M NOT SOUTHERN AND I HAVEN'T EVEN VISITED THE SOUTH, SO IF I WANT A TASTE OF IT, I MAKE CORNBREAD. THIS SKILLET CORNBREAD, TO BE EXACT. IT'S BUTTERY, A LITTLE CRUNCHY AND HAS A BEAUTIFUL BROWN CRUST. IT'S JUST AS AT HOME NEXT TO A MUG OF TEA AS IT IS WITH SOME FRIED EGGS AND BACON — IT'S A BREAKFAST ALL-ROUNDER. AND DON'T FORGET TO SLATHER ON THAT BURNT HONEY BUTTER! IN THE SPIRIT OF SOUTHERN HOSPITALITY, BE GENEROUS WITH IT, YA'LL.*

*SKILLET CORNBREAD*
140 G (5 OZ) BUTTER
150 G (5½ OZ/1 CUP) PLAIN (ALL-PURPOSE) FLOUR
150 G (5½ OZ/1 CUP) POLENTA
55 G (2 OZ/¼ CUP) CASTER (SUPERFINE) SUGAR
2 TEASPOONS BAKING POWDER
1 TEASPOON BICARBONATE OF SODA (BAKING SODA)
PINCH OF SALT
250 ML (8½ FL OZ/1 CUP) BUTTERMILK
125 G (4½ OZ/½ CUP) SOUR CREAM
2 EGGS

*BURNT HONEY BUTTER*
60 ML (2 OZ/¼ CUP) HONEY
100 G (3½ OZ) BUTTER, SOFTENED

To make the burnt honey butter, put the honey in a small saucepan over medium heat. Cook until it begins to darken in colour, and becomes a deep amber. Remove from the heat and set aside to cool completely.

When the honey is completely cool, put the soft butter in a bowl (or in the bowl of a stand mixer with the paddle attachment) and beat in the honey. Scrape into a serving bowl and refrigerate.

To make the cornbread, preheat the oven to 200°C (400°F).

Melt the butter in a 23–25 cm (9–10 in) ovenproof cast-iron skillet or heavy-based frying pan. Use a pastry brush to make sure that the side of the skillet is coated in butter.

Put the remaining cornbread ingredients in a large mixing bowl, pour in the butter and stir everything together with a wooden spoon. Pour the batter back into the buttery skillet and bake for 18–20 minutes, or until golden brown at the edges and springing back when touched lightly. Leave to cool for about 10 minutes before serving warm with the honey butter.

Serves 6–8

# BLUEBERRY PANCAKE GRANOLA

*I am a pancake fiend. In this book alone there are no less than four pancake recipes. But as man cannot live on bread alone, this woman cannot live on pancakes alone (though she wishes she could). Enter, pancake-flavoured granola. This crunchy, buttery, maple-y mix is studded with blueberries and hits all the right flavour notes for a pancake breakfast. But instead of being warm, not at all portable and necessitating a leisurely morning, this granola is crunchy, portable and super-quick to grab. It's also full of good fats and plenty of fibre – bonus!*

200 G (7 OZ/2 CUPS) WHOLE ROLLED (PORRIDGE) OATS
100 G (3½ OZ/1 CUP) QUINOA FLAKES (OR REPLACE WITH ADDITIONAL OATS)
150 G (5½ OZ/1½ CUPS) WHOLE PECANS
45 G (1½ OZ/½ CUP) FLAKED ALMONDS
60 G (2 OZ/½ CUP) CHIA SEEDS
125 ML (4 FL OZ/½ CUP) MAPLE SYRUP
60 ML (2 FL OZ/¼ CUP) RUNNY HONEY
1 TABLESPOON VANILLA BEAN PASTE
1 TEASPOON GROUND CINNAMON
30 G (1 OZ) BUTTER, MELTED (OR COCONUT OIL IS GOOD TOO)
2 TEASPOONS LINSEED (FLAX SEED) OIL (OPTIONAL)
125 G (4½ OZ/1 CUP) DRIED BLUEBERRIES

Preheat the oven to 180°C (350°F) and line two baking trays with baking paper.

Put the oats, quinoa flakes, pecans, almonds and chia seeds in a large bowl and stir to combine.

In a measuring pitcher, whisk together the maple syrup, honey, vanilla, cinnamon, melted butter and linseed oil, if using, until incorporated. Pour the liquid into the dry ingredients and stir together well.

Dump the mixture onto the lined trays and spread out in even layers. Bake for 25 minutes, stirring everything around halfway through baking time, making sure to bring the edges into the middle and vice versa. At the end of baking, the mixture will have browned but may still feel a little soft – don't worry it will crisp up as it cools.

Leave to cool on the trays completely, then stir through the blueberries. Store in an airtight container at room temperature for 1–2 weeks, or in the freezer for up to 3 months.

Makes about 750 g (1 lb 11 oz/6 cups)

*I'M GOING TO PUT IT OUT THERE STRAIGHT AWAY — THIS IS A YORKSHIRE PUDDING THAT YOU EAT FOR BREAKFAST. IF THAT DOESN'T SOUND LIKE THE BEST THING EVER TO YOU, THEN I'M NOT SURE WE CAN BE FRIENDS. THINK OF AN EGGY, MILKY BATTER BEING POURED INTO A HOT PAN AND BAKED UNTIL IT EXPLODES INTO A CRISPY-EDGED, CUSTARD-CENTRED PANCAKE CLOUD. AND THEN YOU RIP OPEN THAT CLOUD, FILL IT WITH CHERRY-BOURBON COMPOTE AND SERVE IT WITH YOGHURT OR CRÈME FRAÎCHE. SPEAKING OF THE COMPOTE, YOU DON'T HAVE TO MAKE IT — YOU COULD EASILY SUBSTITUTE YOUR FAVOURITE POSH JAM. BUT IT'S SO EASY TO PULL TOGETHER, AND ANY LEFTOVERS ARE GORGEOUS ON TOAST OR EVEN WARMED UP AND SERVED OVER ICE CREAM — MAYBE WITH A SCATTERING OF TOASTED ALMONDS. ALSO, IT'S BOURBON AT BREAKFAST. WHAT'S NOT TO LOVE?*

*VANILLA BEAN DUTCH BABY*
25 G (1 OZ) BUTTER
100 G (3½ OZ/⅔ CUP) PLAIN (ALL-PURPOSE) FLOUR
2 TABLESPOONS CASTER (SUPERFINE) SUGAR
PINCH OF SALT
3 EGGS
1 VANILLA BEAN, SPLIT LENGTHWAYS AND SEEDS SCRAPED
190 ML (6½ FL OZ/¾ CUP) MILK

*CHERRY-BOURBON COMPOTE*
400 G (14 OZ/2 CUPS) CHERRIES, PITTED
55 G (2 OZ/¼ CUP) CASTER (SUPERFINE) SUGAR
2 TABLESPOONS BOURBON

To make the cherry–bourbon compote, put all the ingredients in a saucepan and bring to a boil over medium heat. Once the cherries have wilted and become tender, remove them from the pan with a slotted spoon and place in a jar or serving dish.

Reduce the liquid in the pan down to a thin syrup then pour this over the cherries.

To make the Dutch baby, preheat the oven to 200°C (400°F).

Put the butter in a 20–23 cm (8–9 in) ovenproof cast-iron frying pan (or a similar-sized baking dish), then put the pan in the oven to heat up.

In a medium bowl, whisk together the flour, sugar and salt. Whisk in the eggs and vanilla seeds, followed by the milk, making sure there are no lumps.

When the butter in the pan has melted, carefully remove the pan from the oven, pour in the batter and put it straight back in. Bake for 18–20 minutes or until puffed up and golden. Serve straight away with plenty of the compote.

Serves 2

# SWEET POTATO WAFFLES WITH ROSEMARY MAPLE SYRUP

NOWHERE DO THE WORLDS OF SWEET AND SAVOURY COMBINE IN A MORE EXPLOSIVE AND DELICIOUS WAY THAN AT THE BREAKFAST TABLE. THESE WAFFLES ARE MY EXPRESSION OF THAT, AND I EMBRACE IT TOTALLY. THEY'RE BARELY SWEETENED, WITH PURE INTENSE FLAVOUR COMING DIRECTLY FROM THE SWEET POTATOES. THE MAPLE SYRUP IS SMOKY AND AROMATIC AND CARRIES THE ALMOST CITRUSY SCENT OF THE ROSEMARY DELICIOUSLY. AND WHEN THE TWO MEET? HEAVEN. IF YOU LIKE SWEET POTATOES, YOU'LL LOVE THESE WAFFLES.

225 G (8 OZ/1½ CUPS) PLAIN (ALL-PURPOSE) FLOUR
2 TEASPOONS BAKING POWDER
½ TEASPOON BICARBONATE OF SODA (BAKING SODA)
½ TEASPOON SEA SALT FLAKES
2 TABLESPOONS CASTER (SUPERFINE) SUGAR
2 TABLESPOONS BROWN SUGAR
250 ML (8½ FL OZ/1 CUP) BUTTERMILK
250 G (9 OZ/1 CUP) COOKED, MASHED SWEET POTATO
55 G (2 OZ) BUTTER, MELTED
2 EGGS, SEPARATED, PLUS 1 EGG WHITE
MAPLE-GLAZED BACON, TO SERVE (SEE TIP OPPOSITE)

*ROSEMARY MAPLE SYRUP*
250 ML (8½ FL OZ/1 CUP) MAPLE SYRUP
2 ROSEMARY SPRIGS

To make the rosemary maple syrup, put the maple syrup and rosemary in a small saucepan over medium–low heat. Once the syrup is just hot, turn off the heat and set aside to infuse.

To make the waffles, put all the dry ingredients in a large mixing bowl and whisk to combine.

In a pitcher, stir together the buttermilk, mashed sweet potato, melted butter and egg yolks. Pour the sweet potato mixture into the dry ingredients and stir together until just combined.

Put the egg whites in a separate mixing bowl and whisk until stiff peaks form.

Preheat your waffle maker to medium. When the waffle maker is ready, carefully fold the whites into the remaining batter, then cook the waffles according to the manufacturer's instructions. They should be quite brown and well cooked or they will collapse.

Keep the waffles warm in a low oven until all the batter is used. Serve with the warm rosemary maple syrup and maple-glazed bacon – and maybe a little extra butter.

Serves 4

**TIP** The best thing in the world to serve with waffles is crispy maple-glazed bacon. Put an oven-safe cake rack into a foil-lined tin (trust me, the washing up would be terrible without it) and place as much bacon as you like over the cake rack. Bake in a 200°C (400°F) oven for 10–15 minutes, or until just beginning to brown. Brush with maple syrup and bake for about another 5 minutes until golden brown and crisp. YUM.

COFFEE BREAK

Coffee break – these two words are music to my ears. I am a coffee FIEND. At my house we use a French press (frowned upon, I know – but I don't care), and I like it strong, black and with two sugars. If I'm in a café I will order either a latte or a flat white, because I secretly think they're the same thing. But the wildcard element is what I will have to munch on WITH my coffee. The choices are endless.

I love the between-meal snackiness of a coffee break, but I also like that there's an element of ceremony to it. This is no hastily grabbed fistful of almonds eaten at your desk. The coffee break is about forgetting work for fifteen minutes (or longer *wink*) and having a chat with someone. It's a beloved institution.

In Sweden they have ka, both a noun and a verb, which at its most basic means taking a coffee break. But the true translation is more ambiguous. The Swedes embrace the bonding and cosiness that an intentionally social coffee break can bring. On the same wavelength are those lovely Brits with their afternoon tea – sometimes incredibly formal, but sometimes as simple as a scone and a mug of milky English Breakfast.

A cookie, a brownie, a pastry or a dainty cake; this chapter is a list of all the things that I most want to appear next to my mid-morning cup. Well these and, let's be honest, some gossip. I've done a little globe-trotting here, stopping by the Middle East for bright green Pistachio baklava (page 38) and tripping across the pond for Strawberry and rose butterfly cakes (page 40). But I landed squarely back in Oz with my Homemade Tim Tams (page 42). They, like the elusive coffee break, are not to be missed.

*REMEMBER CHOCOLATE CRACKLES? IF YOU'RE A KID WHO GREW UP IN THE '90S (AND EARLIER, I'M TOLD), I BET A PLATE OF THESE APPEARED AT EVERY BIRTHDAY PARTY AND BRING-A-PLATE EVENT YOU EVER ATTENDED. THE ORIGINAL RECIPE CALLS FOR A WEIRD KIND OF HYDROGENATED COCONUT OIL, ALONG WITH COCOA POWDER, CRISPED RICE CEREAL AND DESICCATED COCONUT. AS A KID, I ABSOLUTELY LOVED THEM. AS AN ADULT, I LOVE THE IDEA, BUT I ALSO WANTED TO SKIP THE HUGE WHITE BLOCK OF FAT AND PUNCH 'EM UP A LITTLE. I GIVE YOU, THE LUXE CRACKLE!*

230 G (8 OZ/1 CUP) CASTER (SUPERFINE) SUGAR
125 ML (4 FL OZ/½ CUP) THICKENED (WHIPPING) CREAM (35% FAT)
125 G (4½ OZ) BUTTER
1 TEASPOON SEA SALT FLAKES
100 G (3½ OZ) MILK CHOCOLATE (50–60% COCOA SOLIDS)
100 G (3½ OZ) DARK CHOCOLATE (70–80% COCOA SOLIDS)
120 G (4½ OZ/4 CUPS) PUFFED RICE CEREAL

Put the sugar and about 60 ml (2 fl oz/¼ cup) water in a deep heavy-based saucepan over medium heat. Cook, without stirring, until the sugar melts and the mixture begins to bubble. If the sugar is melting unevenly, you can tilt and swirl the pan gently, but do not stir. Once the mixture begins to bubble, continue cooking for 5–8 minutes until the sugar darkens to an amber colour – you might see some wisps of smoke rising from the pan, but that's normal.

Remove the pan from the heat and carefully pour in the cream. It will bubble up furiously, but just leave it to settle. Add the butter and salt and cook over low heat, stirring, until everything melts and combines into a gorgeous caramel, about 30 seconds. Leave to cool for 5 minutes.

While you are waiting for the caramel to cool, break up the chocolate into small pieces, put the puffed rice in a large bowl and line a 20 cm (8 in) square tin with baking paper.

When the 5 minutes is up, pour out 60 ml (2 fl oz/¼ cup) of the still-hot caramel and set aside. Add the chocolate to the remaining caramel and stir gently for a few minutes until the chocolate melts.

Pour the melted chocolate and caramel mixture over the rice cereal and stir until everything is combined.

Press the mixture into your lined tin. Drizzle over the remaining caramel and place the tin in the refrigerator to set for at least 2 hours. Cut into pieces and serve.

Makes 12–16 pieces

# SUPER-SOAKED LEMON, ALMOND AND POPPY CAKE

*THIS MIGHT SEEM LIKE A PLAIN CAKE, BUT IT PACKS A HUGE FLAVOUR PUNCH. THERE IS SOME CRAZY, ALCHEMICAL PROCESS THAT OCCURS WHEN YOU BAKE A BUTTERY CAKE WITH ALMONDS, THEN DOUSE IT IN LEMON SYRUP. THE WHOLE THING COMES TO LIFE IN YOUR MOUTH – THE BUTTER TASTES MORE BUTTERY, THE LEMON MORE LEMONY AND THE ALMONDS MORE INTENSE. AND I'M JUST CRAZY ABOUT POPPY SEEDS. THIS CAKE IS PRETTY ORDINARY-LOOKING, BUT WITH A DOLLOP OF CRÈME FRAÎCHE (CHECK, YOU'VE GOT SOME ANYWAY) AND A PILE OF BERRIES ON THE SIDE, THIS IS A PERFECT DESSERT FOR A LONG LUNCH OR A CASUAL DINNER. OR JUST DO AS I DO, AND EAT IT WITH YOUR HANDS, SLICE BY TINY SLICE, HUNCHED OVER THE SINK – NO TIME FOR A PLATE! – UNTIL THERE'S NONE LEFT.*

225 G (8 OZ) BUTTER, AT ROOM TEMPERATURE
230 G (8 OZ/1 CUP) CASTER (SUPERFINE) SUGAR
GRATED ZEST OF 2 LEMONS
4 EGGS
90 G (3 OZ/1/3 CUP) CRÈME FRAÎCHE OR SOUR CREAM
100 G (3½ OZ/1 CUP) ALMOND MEAL
150 G (5½ OZ/1 CUP) PLAIN (ALL-PURPOSE) FLOUR
2 TEASPOONS BAKING POWDER
40 G (1½ OZ/¼ CUP) POPPY SEEDS
80 G (2¾ OZ/½ CUP) ALMONDS, CHOPPED

*SYRUP*
JUICE OF 4 LEMONS
250 G (9 OZ/2 CUPS) ICING (CONFECTIONERS') SUGAR

Preheat the oven to 180°C (350°F) and grease and line a 20–23 cm (8–9 in) springform cake tin.

Beat the butter, sugar and lemon zest together until pale and fluffy. Add the eggs, one at a time, beating well after each addition. Add the crème fraîche and beat again until incorporated. Add the almond meal, flour, baking powder and poppy seeds, and fold until everything is combined.

Pour the mixture into the lined tin and smooth the top. Scatter the chopped almonds over the top of the cake and press them in gently. Bake for 35–40 minutes or until the cake springs back when touched lightly and a skewer comes out clean.

While the cake is baking, stir together the ingredients for the syrup until the icing sugar dissolves.

When the cake is ready, poke a bunch of holes in the top with a skewer (trying to avoid the almonds) and then pour the syrup over the cake. It will seem like too much syrup, but that's the point, so go slowly and keep pouring until all the syrup is absorbed. Let the cake cool completely and then carefully remove from the tin, slice and eat.

Serves 6–8

TIP Check your teeth for poppy seeds after you eat this. That's not a cooking tip, just some helpful advice.

You know the song that tiny guy sings at the start of Aladdin, 'Arabian Niiiiiiights'? That's what plays in my head whenever I make, eat or think about this pistachio baklava – not only because baklava is eaten across the Middle East and into the Mediterranean, but because a lot of the world's pistachio nuts are grown there. Now, pistachio nuts aren't cheap, I know that. That's why this is a small batch, as opposed to a hulking tray of baklava – but you can easily sub in another nut for half the pistachio nuts, or even all of them if you need to. I love to use pistachio nuts, though, because they're so beautiful and the taste is so distinctive. There is a real sense of luxuriousness and decadence to these treats, particularly with their aromatic syrup bath.

150 G (5½ OZ/1 CUP) SHELLED, UNSALTED PISTACHIO NUTS
PINCH OF GROUND CINNAMON
10 SHEETS OF FILO PASTRY
75 G (2¾ OZ) BUTTER, MELTED

*SYRUP*
145 G (5 OZ/⅔ CUP) CASTER (SUPERFINE) SUGAR
170 ML (5½ FL OZ/⅔ CUP) WATER
125 ML (4 FL OZ/½ CUP) HONEY
½ TEASPOON ROSEWATER

To make the syrup, place all the ingredients in a deep saucepan over medium heat and slowly bring to a simmer. Simmer for 8–10 minutes, or until reduced by a third. Remove from the heat, leave to cool completely, then chill in the refrigerator.

Preheat the oven to 180°C (350°F).

For the filling, blitz the pistachio nuts and cinnamon in a food processor to a medium–fine texture – lots of dusty rubble, with a few bigger pieces.

Lay a sheet of filo pastry out on a clean work surface and brush with some of the melted butter. Cover with a second sheet and brush again. Take about a sixth of the pistachio nuts and sprinkle them evenly along the short edge of the pastry. Roll the pastry up tightly into a log, and cut into 5 even pieces – if some of the nuts fall out, don't worry about it. Brush a 23 cm (9 in) flan (tart) tin with butter, and begin laying the baklava pieces in a circular pattern.

Continue the process with the remaining pastry and the nut mixture until the tin is full, and all the pastry is used up. You should have about a sixth of the nuts left over.

Once all the baklava is in the tin, brush with the remaining melted butter and bake for 15 minutes, or until golden brown.

Remove the baklava from the oven and transfer to a baking tray. Immediately spoon the chilled syrup over the hot baklava, soaking each piece. Decorate with the extra nuts. Leave to soak and cool for an hour, then serve.

*Makes 25 pieces*

# STRAWBERRY AND ROSE BUTTERFLY CAKES

*A TENDER LITTLE BUTTERCAKE, FILLED WITH ROSE-SCENTED STRAWBERRY JAM AND A DOLLOP OF WHIPPED CRÈME FRAÎCHE. IF YOU KNOW ANY FAIRY-OBSESSED CHILDREN, ADULTS OR JUST ANYONE WHO YOU CAN TRICK INTO HAVING AN OUTRAGEOUSLY PINK TEA PARTY, THESE ARE THE CAKES TO BAKE. THEY ARE ELEGANT AND SOMEHOW EXTRA-SPECIAL – TO MY MIND THESE COMPLETELY ECLIPSE CUPCAKES WHICH, LET'S FACE IT, ARE TOTALLY PLAYED OUT. I LOVE THE WAY THE WINGS JUT OUT ON TOP, MAKING THESE LOOK LIKE THEY COULD TAKE OFF AT ANY MOMENT.*

150 G (5½ OZ/1 CUP) PLAIN (ALL-PURPOSE) FLOUR
2 TEASPOONS BAKING POWDER
115 G (4 OZ/½ CUP) CASTER (SUPERFINE) SUGAR
100 G (3½ OZ) BUTTER, SOFTENED
2 EGGS
1 TEASPOON VANILLA BEAN PASTE
½ TEASPOON FRESHLY GRATED NUTMEG
2 TABLESPOONS MILK
105 G (3½ OZ/⅓ CUP) STRAWBERRY JAM
½ TEASPOON ROSEWATER, OR TO TASTE
125 G (4½ OZ/½ CUP) CRÈME FRAÎCHE OR SOUR CREAM
60 ML (2 FL OZ/¼ CUP) THICKENED (WHIPPING) CREAM (35% FAT)
ICING (CONFECTIONERS') SUGAR, TO DUST

Preheat the oven to 180°C (350°F) and line a cupcake tray with 12 paper cases.

Put the flour, baking powder, sugar and butter in a large bowl (or in the bowl of a stand mixer fitted with the paddle attachment). Beat until the mixture looks like fine breadcrumbs. Continue beating, adding the eggs, one at a time, until the mixture comes together in a thick batter. Add the vanilla, nutmeg and milk and beat until just incorporated.

Distribute the batter evenly between the paper cases. Bake for 20 minutes, or until golden and the cakes spring back when touched lightly. Set aside to cool completely on a wire rack.

While the cakes are cooling, stir the jam and rosewater together in a small bowl (taste and add more rosewater, if you like).

Whip the crème fraîche and cream together until thick.

Using a small sharp knife, carefully cut the top off each cake, digging into the cake to leave a little divot. Fill each cupcake with a tiny splodge of jam, spreading it over the cut surface, followed by a bigger splodge of whipped cream. Take a cake top, slice it in two and stick the pieces into the cream on the cake, to look like wings. Dust the cakes with icing sugar and serve.

Makes 12

THE QUESTION WAS NOT WHETHER I COULD MAKE TIM TAMS AT HOME, BUT WHETHER I SHOULD. I MEAN, THAT LITTLE MALTY CHOCOLATE SANDWICH COOKIE IS AN AUSTRALIAN ICON (SIMILAR TO A PENGUIN BISCUIT, IF YOU'RE IN THE UK). COULD THE ORIGINAL ARTICLE BE IMPROVED ON? THERE IS A REASON THAT PEOPLE ALWAYS WISH FOR A NEVER-ENDING PACKET OF TIM TAMS, AND THAT'S BECAUSE THEY'RE GREAT … BUT COULD THEY BE MALTIER? MORE CHOCOLATEY? COULD THE CHOCOLATE COATING BE THICKER? THE ANSWER TO ALL THREE IS YES!

115 G (4 OZ) BUTTER, SOFTENED
115 G (4 OZ/½ CUP) CASTER (SUPERFINE) SUGAR
1 EGG
30 G (1 OZ/¼ CUP) UNSWEETENED (DUTCH) COCOA POWDER
150 G (5½ OZ/1 CUP) PLAIN (ALL-PURPOSE) FLOUR
PINCH OF SALT

*FILLING*
115 G (4 OZ) BUTTER
125 G (4½ OZ/1 CUP) ICING (CONFECTIONERS') SUGAR
1 TABLESPOON UNSWEETENED (DUTCH) COCOA POWDER
1 TABLESPOON MALTED DRINK POWDER (SUCH AS OVALTINE OR HORLICKS)

*COATING*
200 G (7 OZ) MILK CHOCOLATE (60% COCOA SOLIDS)
1 TABLESPOON COCONUT OIL

Cream together the butter and sugar until pale and fluffy. Scrape down the bowl, add the egg and continue beating until the egg is incorporated and the mixture lightens in colour. Add the cocoa powder and beat until there are no lumps. Finally, fold through the flour and salt until it is all incorporated. The dough will be very soft. Turn the dough out onto a piece of baking paper on a work surface, top with another piece of baking paper and roll out to a large rectangle about 5 mm (¼ in) thick. Put the dough on a tray and put it in the freezer for 30 minutes.

Preheat the oven to 180°C (350°F) and line two baking trays with baking paper.

Take the dough out of the freezer and slice it into 28 small 3 x 6 cm (1¼ x 2½ in) rectangles. Separate the rectangles and spread them out on the lined baking trays. Bake for 10 minutes, then transfer to a wire rack to cool completely.

To make the filling, cream the butter until soft, sift in the remaining ingredients and beat until well combined. Spread a heaped teaspoon of filling on half the cookies. Top with the remaining cookies, then put in the refrigerator to chill, while you make the coating.

For the coating, place the chocolate and coconut oil in a heat-proof bowl and melt together in the microwave on High (100%) in 30-second bursts, stirring well after each burst. Once the chocolate is mostly melted, remove and stir gently until smooth.

Take a chilled cookie and carefully coat it in the chocolate – this is easiest if you use your hands – then put it on a lined baking tray. Chill in the refrigerator, then try and stop yourself from eating them all immediately!

*Makes 14*

# MAPLE PECAN BEAR CLAWS

*OH, CANADA. IN SO MANY WAYS YOU FEEL LIKE THE SISTER COUNTRY TO US HERE IN AUSTRALIA – ANOTHER ENGLISH-SPEAKING NATION THAT OFTEN FLIES UNDER THE RADAR ON THE WORLD STAGE. WE BOTH HAVE ACCENTS THAT TEND TO CONFUSE PEOPLE (BRITISH, IRISH, KIWI?). YOU GAVE THE WORLD MAPLE SYRUP AND YOU'RE HOME TO MY SPIRIT ANIMAL, THE BROWN BEAR. LET'S EAT A BEAR CLAW TOGETHER, CANADA.*

*PASTRY*
300 G (10½ OZ/2 CUPS) PLAIN (ALL-PURPOSE) FLOUR
1 TEASPOON DRY ACTIVE YEAST
125 ML (4 FL OZ/½ CUP) WARM WATER
1 EGG
200 G (7 OZ) BUTTER

*FILLING*
75 G (2¾ OZ) BUTTER, SOFTENED
55 G (2 OZ/¼ CUP) CASTER (SUPERFINE) SUGAR
1 TEASPOON PURE MAPLE EXTRACT (SEE TIP OPPOSITE)
1 EGG YOLK, PLUS 1 BEATEN EGG FOR BRUSHING
55 G (2 OZ/½ CUP) ALMOND MEAL
2 TABLESPOONS PLAIN (ALL-PURPOSE) FLOUR
60 G (2 OZ/½ CUP) CHOPPED PECANS

To make the pastry, in a medium mixing bowl (or the bowl of a stand mixer, with the dough hook attached) combine the flour, yeast, warm water and egg. Mix the ingredients together until they form a dough. Transfer the dough to a floured work surface and knead for about 10 minutes (or simply knead for 5 minutes in the mixer), until the dough is smooth and elastic. Cover with plastic wrap and leave in a warm place for an hour or until doubled in size.

Once the dough has risen, lightly flour a work surface and roll into a 30 x 40 cm (12 x 16 in) rectangle, with the short side facing you. Slice the butter thinly and lay the butter in the middle half of the dough, leaving a quarter of the dough exposed at the top and bottom. Fold the top and bottom pieces of dough over the butter, so they meet in the middle and the butter is covered. Then, fold the right and left hand edges of the dough to meet in the middle, and fold the whole thing in half, so the seam is on the left. Press the dough firmly down to seal it, and then roll it back out to 30 x 40 cm (12 x 16 in). Repeat the same folding process twice more. Wrap tightly in plastic wrap and chill in the refrigerator for 2 hours or overnight

Preheat the oven to 180°C (350°F) and line a baking tray with baking paper.

Make the filling by beating together the butter, sugar, maple extract, egg yolk, almond meal and flour, until well combined. Fold through the pecans.

Take the dough out of the refrigerator and cut it into 2 pieces. Roll one out into a 16 x 32 cm (6¼ x 12¾ in) rectangle, then cut it into four 8 x 16 cm (3¼ x 6¼ in) rectangles. Put 1 tablespoon of filling in the middle of each. Brush the edges with beaten egg and fold the pastry over to seal. Put the bear claws on the baking tray, cut 'toes' into the side of each bear claw, brush again with egg. Set aside to rise for 15 minutes. Repeat with the other piece of dough.

Bake the bear claws for 25–30 minutes or until deep golden brown and crisp. Serve warm with coffee.

*Makes 8*

**TIP** If you can't get hold of pure maple extract, you can get the same maple flavour by using maple sugar instead of regular caster (superfine) sugar.

# HONEY ALMOND MADELEINES

*THERE IS A VERY FAMOUS WRITER WHO ONCE MENTIONED MADELEINES IN HIS WORK. AND THEN FOR THE NEXT 100 YEARS, EVERY FOOD WRITER IN THE WORLD WOULDN'T STOP MENTIONING IT. I'VE MADE IT MY PROFESSIONAL MISSION TO NEVER USE THAT PARTICULAR MADELEINE STORY, AND I'M NOT ABOUT TO START, BECAUSE I DON'T THINK THESE LITTLE COOKIE-CAKES NEED THE HELP. THEY ARE TENDER, SHELL-SHAPED, MINIATURE CAKES, RICH WITH BROWNED BUTTER (THE SECRET WEAPON), SCENTED WITH HONEY (PICK A STRONG ONE) AND SERVED WARM, STRAIGHT FROM THE OVEN. SCREW PROUST, LET'S BAKE!*

100 G (3½ OZ) BUTTER, PLUS EXTRA TO GREASE
2 EGGS
80 G (2¾ OZ/⅓ CUP) CASTER (SUPERFINE) SUGAR
1 TABLESPOON HONEY, PLUS EXTRA TO SERVE
100 G (3½ OZ/⅔ CUP) PLAIN (ALL-PURPOSE) FLOUR
½ TEASPOON BAKING POWDER
2 TABLESPOONS ALMONDS, FINELY CHOPPED

Preheat the oven to 200°C (400°F) and brush a non-stick madeleine tin liberally with butter.

Melt the butter in a small saucepan over medium–low heat, then continue to cook the butter until it foams up, turns a golden brown colour and begins to smell nutty. This will take about 4–5 minutes all up. Once the butter is browned, take it off the heat, pour it into a small bowl and leave it to cool.

Put the eggs, sugar and honey in a large mixing bowl and whisk on high speed (or use a stand mixer fitted with the whisk attachment) until they have doubled in volume, and become mousse-y and pale. With the mixer on medium speed, stream in the butter and whisk until incorporated. Turn off the mixer and stir through the flour and baking powder.

Spoon the batter into the madeleine tin, filling each indent about two-thirds full (you may need to do two or even three batches, depending on the size of your tin). Scatter over a light layer of the almonds and bake for 7–10 minutes, or until golden brown and the madeleines spring back when touched lightly. Serve warm, drizzled with extra honey.

Makes 12 large madeleines

# CHOC CHIP PRETZEL COOKIES

*THIS IS MY COOKIE MASTERPIECE — ONE OF THE MOST POPULAR RECIPES I'VE EVER PUBLISHED ON MY BLOG. I ABSOLUTELY ADORE THESE COOKIES AND I THINK THE WORLD NEEDS MORE OF THEM. THEY ARE BITTER AND SWEET, CHEWY AND CRUNCHY, SALTY AND CARAMELLY, AND EVERYTHING I'VE EVER WANTED IN MY LIFE. YOU WANT THESE IN YOUR LIFE TOO. TRUST ME.*

125 G (4½ OZ) BUTTER, AT ROOM TEMPERATURE
230 G (8 OZ/1 CUP, FIRMLY PACKED) BROWN SUGAR
2 TABLESPOONS CASTER (SUPERFINE) SUGAR
2 TABLESPOONS RAW (DEMERARA) SUGAR
1 EGG
2 TEASPOONS VANILLA BEAN PASTE
260 G (9 OZ/1¾ CUPS) PLAIN (ALL-PURPOSE) FLOUR
½ TEASPOON BAKING POWDER
100 G (3½ OZ/1 CUP) SALTED PRETZELS, PLUS 15 EXTRA FOR TOPPING
200 G (7 OZ/1⅓ CUPS) CHOPPED DARK CHOCOLATE (70% COCOA SOLIDS)

Preheat the oven to 180°C (350°F) and line two baking trays with baking paper.

Put the butter and sugars in a bowl and cream for at least 5 minutes until pale and fluffy. Scrape down the bowl and add the egg, then beat again until the egg is completely incorporated. Scrape down the bowl, add the vanilla and beat again.

In a small bowl, stir together the flour and baking powder, then gradually add to the butter mixture, stirring slowly until the flour is almost completely incorporated.

Crush the pretzels in your hands gently, just to break them roughly into quarters. Add them to the dough, along with the chopped chocolate. Fold the dough together with a wooden spoon or spatula just until everything is incorporated and the chocolate and pretzels are evenly distributed.

Scoop ¼ cup sized portions of dough out, and roll them gently in your hands before placing them onto the lined baking trays. Make sure there is plenty of room between the cookies, because they spread to at least twice the uncooked size. Put a whole pretzel onto each dough ball and press gently to slightly flatten the cookie and embed the pretzel in the dough. Bake the cookies for 12 minutes, rotating the trays halfway through baking. The cookies will spread and be set at the edges, but still look a little gooey in the centre. Leave to cool on the trays, then eat them! A glass of milk on the side is mandatory.

**Makes 15**

THESE MUFFINS ARE MY HOMAGE TO NEW YORK, BABY! THEY'RE BIG, THEY'RE FULL OF APPLE (GEDDIT, BIG APPLE?) AND THEY'RE INSPIRED BY THE INSTITUTION THAT IS THE NEW YORK CRUMB CAKE, WHICH MAKES THEM PERFECT FOR SNACKING ON. THEY MAKE ME THINK OF SASSY, BRASSY, OLD NEW YORK WOMEN WITH NAMES LIKE ETHEL AND ROSE, WHO WEAR WAY TOO MUCH CHUNKY JEWELLERY AND HEAD DOWN TO THE BAKERY EVERY SATURDAY MORNING FOR A LOUD, SHOUTY CATCH-UP OVER CAKE.

```
100 G (3½ OZ) BUTTER
230 G (8 OZ/1 CUP) CASTER (SUPERFINE) SUGAR
1 EGG
250 ML (8½ FL OZ/1 CUP) BUTTERMILK
1 TEASPOON VANILLA BEAN PASTE
300 G (10½ OZ/2 CUPS) PLAIN (ALL-PURPOSE) FLOUR
½ TEASPOON BAKING POWDER
1 TEASPOON BICARBONATE OF SODA (BAKING SODA)
PINCH OF SALT
2 APPLES (CHOOSE A TART VARIETY), PEELED AND CUT INTO 1 CM (½ IN) DICE
```

```
CRUMB TOPPING
175 G (6 OZ) BUTTER
155 G (5½ OZ/⅔ CUP, FIRMLY PACKED) BROWN SUGAR
45 G (1½ OZ) CASTER (SUPERFINE) SUGAR
1 TEASPOON SALT
2 TEASPOONS GROUND CINNAMON
300 G (10½ OZ/2 CUPS) PLAIN (ALL-PURPOSE) FLOUR
```

Preheat the oven to 175°C (345°F). Grease twelve 190 ml (6½ fl oz/¾ cup) capacity ramekins, or line a large, 12-hole muffin tin with large muffin cases.

To make the crumb topping, melt the butter in a small bowl in the microwave on High (100%) for 30 seconds. Add the butter to the remaining ingredients in a mixing bowl and stir together until combined. Set aside.

Cream together the butter and sugar until pale and fluffy. Add the egg and beat until completely incorporated. Add the remaining ingredients and stir until everything is combined and homogenous, being careful not to over-mix.

Divide the batter evenly between the ramekins or muffin cases, then top them equally with the crumb mixture – squeeze together big pieces of the mix, then crumble them over each muffin to get nice big chunks.

Put the ramekins on a baking tray and bake for 25–30 minutes, or until a skewer inserted into a muffin comes out clean. Leave to cool slightly, before carefully removing from the ramekins or the tin and serving. These are particularly delicious when they're still a bit warm.

Makes 12

**TIP** You need BIG muffin cases for these babies – they are definitely larger than your average muffin. Most supermarkets sell large muffin cases (I like the ones that look like they're made of brown paper). But if you can't get them, you can use regular cases – you'll just end up with more, smaller muffins. Alternatively, you can bake them in mini-panettone moulds or make your own cases using baking paper.

YOU KNOW WHAT I LOVE? BROWNIES. AND THE RECIPE BELOW IS THE *ULTIMATE* BROWNIE BATTER. WHY GARBAGE BROWNIES? THESE BROWNIES WILL TAKE WHATEVER GARBAGE YOU WANT TO THROW AT THEM, AND THEY WILL STILL BAKE BEAUTIFULLY AND TURN OUT LIKE HEAVEN. THE COCOA-BASED BATTER IS SO EASY-GOING, AND BAKES UP INTO A CHEWY, RICH, DENSE MASTERPIECE NO MATTER WHAT YOU DO TO IT. AS IF YOU NEEDED ANY MORE ENCOURAGEMENT, YOU PROBABLY ALREADY HAVE ALL THE INGREDIENTS IN YOUR CUPBOARD. ON THE OPPOSITE PAGE ARE TWO OF MY FAVOURITE VARIATIONS. THE PEANUT BUTTER POPCORN BROWNIES ARE A HUGE, RIDICULOUS, POPCORN-COVERED MESS. I LOVE BAKING THESE IN A CIRCULAR TIN BECAUSE THEY CUT MORE EASILY INTO WEDGES THAN THEY WOULD INTO SQUARES – BUT, REALLY, WE ALL KNOW THAT NEATNESS IS NOT THE ENDGAME HERE. THEN THERE ARE THE S'MORES BROWNIES – COOKIE, CHOCOLATE AND TOASTED MARSHMALLOW – ALL CRAMMED INTO BROWNIES. THE BASE IS BUTTERY, THE CENTRE IS CHEWY AND DELICIOUS AND THE MARSHMALLOWS ARE JUST AS TOASTY AS THEY OUGHT TO BE. THE AWESOMENESS OF THESE BROWNIES NEED NO FURTHER EXPLANATION. BUT PLEASE, NO COLOURED MARSHMALLOWS. IT'LL LOOK LIKE A UNICORN THREW UP ON YOUR BROWNIES.

# GARBAGE BROWNIES

150 G (5½ OZ) BUTTER
285 G (10 OZ/1¼ CUPS) CASTER (SUPERFINE) SUGAR
90 G (3 OZ/¾ CUP) UNSWEETENED (DUTCH) COCOA POWDER
1 TEASPOON VANILLA BEAN PASTE
PINCH OF SEA SALT
2 EGGS
50 G (1¾ OZ/⅓ CUP) PLAIN (ALL-PURPOSE) FLOUR
WHATEVER EXTRA MIX-INS YOU WANT!

Preheat the oven to 160°C (320°F). Grease and line a 20 cm (8 in) square tin with baking paper, letting the paper overhang the sides of the tin.

Melt the butter in a large saucepan over medium heat. Take the pan off the heat and add the sugar and cocoa, stirring until there are no lumps. Add the vanilla, salt and eggs and stir again until everything is combined. Finally add the flour, stir until combined then continue beating vigorously with a wooden spoon for about 30 seconds until the mixture comes together in a smooth, shiny batter. If it looks separated or greasy, keep beating until it comes together.

For standard, chewy, gooey chocolate brownies, scrape the batter into the tin and bake for 20 minutes. But if you want to get creative with mix-ins now's the time! There are no bad choices here – throw in any nuts, candy, berries, fruit, seeds or other goodness that your heart desires, and then proceed to scrape the batter into the tin and bake as above. Cool in the tin, then slice into 16 pieces. They keep well for up to a week in an airtight container.

Makes 16 pieces

# PEANUT BUTTER POPCORN BROWNIES

1 BATCH GARBAGE BROWNIES BATTER (SEE OPPOSITE PAGE)
125 G (4¹/₂ OZ/¹/₂ CUP) PEANUT BUTTER
100 G (3¹/₂ OZ) DARK CHOCOLATE (70% COCOA SOLIDS), MELTED
45 G (1¹/₂ OZ/3 CUPS) BUTTERED POPCORN

Preheat the oven to 160°C (320°F) and grease and line a 23 cm (9 in) round cake tin with baking paper, letting the paper overhang the side of the tin.

Pour the batter into the tin, then dollop over the peanut butter in teaspoon-sized blobs. Using a skewer or butter knife, swirl the peanut butter through the batter. Bake for 25–30 minutes, or until smooth and shiny on the surface with no wobble to the batter. Set aside to cool completely in the tin.

Drizzle a little of the melted chocolate over the cooled brownie, then scatter over a layer of popcorn, followed by more chocolate and more popcorn until both are used up. The chocolate will firm up and glue the popcorn in place. Leave to set completely, then slice and serve.

Makes 12

# S'MORES BROWNIES

250 G (9 OZ) BUTTERNUT SNAP COOKIES (OR DIGESTIVES OR GRAHAM CRACKERS)
50 G (1³/₄ OZ) BUTTER, SOFTENED
1 BATCH GARBAGE BROWNIES BATTER (SEE OPPOSITE PAGE)
90 G (3 OZ/2 CUPS) VANILLA MINI-MARSHMALLOWS
   OR 90 G (3 OZ/1 CUP) VANILLA MARSHMALLOWS

Preheat the oven to 160°C (320°F) and grease and line a 20 cm (8 in) square tin with baking paper, letting the paper overhang the sides of the tin.

Blitz the cookies and butter in a food processor until they form a fine, sandy crumb.

Press the mixture firmly into the tin. Pour over the batter, then scatter over the mini-marshmallows. Bake for 25 minutes, then leave to cool completely in the tin before lifting out and cutting into squares.

Makes 16

PEANUT BUTTER
POPCORN BROWNIES

# HEALTHY JUNK

I'M GOING TO TELL YOU SOMETHING THAT MAY SHOCK YOU - I'M A LITTLE BIT GREEDY. I DON'T LIKE A DAY TO GO BY WHERE I DON'T GET TO ENJOY SOME ILLICIT TREAT. HAVING SAID THAT, I'M ALSO NOT CRAZY, AND I STILL WANT TO FIT INTO MY JEANS. THAT'S WHERE THE RECIPES IN THIS CHAPTER COME IN. HEALTHY JUNK! SUPERCHARGED RECIPES, WHICH ARE ALL TOTALLY DELICIOUS AND HIT THAT SWEET SPOT, BUT WITH A TURBO BOOST. IT MIGHT BE REFINED SUGAR-FREE, OR CHOCK FULL OF FIBRE, HEALTHY FATS AND VITAMINS. SOMETIMES IT'S JUST A BIG OLD SERVING OF FRUIT, PIMPED OUT WITH HERBS, OR A FROZEN ELEMENT, OR MAYBE EVEN SOMETHING FROM THE DRINKS CABINET. WHATEVER THAT ADDED EXTRA IS, IT MAKES ME FEEL TOTALLY VIRTUOUS AND BRIMMING WITH HEALTH.

THE OTHER GREAT THING ABOUT THESE RECIPES IS THAT THEY'RE VERY WELCOMING. PEOPLE MAKE DECISIONS ABOUT THEIR DIET BASED ON ALL SORTS OF DIFFERENT REASONS. A LOT OF THE TIME THAT MEANS CUTTING SOMETHING OUT AND A LOT OF THE TIME IT'S NOT BY CHOICE. I LOVE BEING ABLE TO HAVE THOSE PEOPLE OVER AND STILL OFFER THEM SOMETHING DELICIOUS, REGARDLESS OF WHO'S AVOIDING DAIRY OR GLUTEN OR ANIMAL PRODUCTS.

BUT SPEAKING AS SOMEONE WHO EMBRACES DAIRY, REVELS IN GLUTEN AND WILL NEVER STOP EATING BACON, I CAN GUARANTEE THE DELICIOUSNESS OF THESE RECIPES. I WOULDN'T HAVE PUT THEM IN HERE IF I THOUGHT THERE WAS SOMETHING BETTER I COULD HAVE REPLACED THEM WITH. I WILL TAKE A RASPBERRY COCONUT YOGHURT POP (PAGE 64) ANY DAY, AND I HAVE TO RATION OUT MY CHEWY COCOA DATE FUDGE (PAGE 74) WHENEVER I MAKE IT. I HOPE YOU TRY THESE OUT, ENJOY THEM AND FEEL GREAT ABOUT IT TOO!

# ALMOND OAT PORRIDGE WITH ROAST PEACHES

*THIS RECIPE IS VEGAN, WHOLEGRAIN AND REFINED SUGAR-FREE. IT'S ALSO CREAMY, SWEET AND DECADENT. IT'S A GENUINE MIRACLE WHEN THOSE THINGS ALL OCCUR IN THE SAME BOWL OF FOOD AND, AS FAR AS I'M CONCERNED, THAT'S A GOOD ENOUGH REASON TO EAT THIS CONSTANTLY FOR AS LONG AS PEACHES ARE IN SEASON. AND PLEASE DON'T LET THE WORD 'PORRIDGE' PUT YOU OFF. I KNOW IT CAN CONJURE UP IMAGES OF GREY, GLUEY PASTES, BUT THIS IS COMPLETELY DIFFERENT. INSTEAD OF CHARLES DICKENS AND THIN GRUEL, THINK TARTAN BLANKETS, WINDSWEPT MOORS AND A MAGICAL HOT BREAKFAST BOWL, WHICH IS SOMEHOW BOTH LUXURIOUS AND GREAT FOR YOU.*

## ROAST PEACHES
2 LARGE YELLOW PEACHES
2–4 TABLESPOONS MAPLE SYRUP
1 TABLESPOON COCONUT OIL OR BUTTER, MELTED

## PORRIDGE
100 G (3½ OZ/1 CUP) WHOLE ROLLED (PORRIDGE) OATS
80 G (2¾ OZ/½ CUP) ALMONDS, COARSELY CHOPPED
625 ML (21 FL OZ/2½ CUPS) ALMOND MILK
PINCH OF SALT
PINCH OF GROUND CINNAMON, TO SERVE

Preheat the oven to 200°C (400°F).

Wash the peaches and cut them into quarters, removing the stones. Slice a tiny piece of peach for yourself and taste it for sweetness.

Put the peach pieces in a shallow baking dish and toss with the maple syrup and coconut oil, adding as much syrup as you think the peaches need. Roast them for 20 minutes, tossing them gently halfway through, or until they are tender and a little blistered.

While the peaches are cooking, make the porridge. Put the oats, most of the almonds (save some for sprinkling over your porridge), the almond milk and salt in a large saucepan over low heat. Cook, stirring, for around 10 minutes or until the porridge is thick and silky.

To serve, divide the porridge between two bowls, pile on the peaches, scatter over the remaining almonds and sprinkle with the cinnamon.

Serves 2

# SUPER-EASY CHERRY HAZELNUT ENERGY BARS

*THESE BARS ARE EXACTLY THE ENERGY BOOST I NEED, WHETHER I'M ROAD TRIPPIN', GOING FOR A LONG WALK, OR SITTING AT MY DESK FRANTICALLY TRYING TO FINISH WRITING THIS BOOK. THE RECIPE IS SO SIMPLE, THE INGREDIENTS ARE ALL EASY TO COME BY AND THE TASTE IS COMPLETELY DELICIOUS. THESE ARE A SNACK-LOVER'S SAVIOUR.*

100 G (3½ OZ/1 CUP) WHOLE ROLLED (PORRIDGE) OATS
50 G (1¾ OZ/½ CUP) PECANS, CHOPPED
60 G (2 OZ/½ CUP) SLIVERED ALMONDS
70 G (2½ OZ/½ CUP) HAZELNUTS
45 G (1½ OZ/½ CUP) DESICCATED COCONUT
75 G (2¾ OZ/½ CUP) DRIED CHERRIES
80 ML (2½ FL OZ/⅓ CUP) HONEY
55 G (2 OZ/¼ CUP, FIRMLY PACKED) DARK MUSCOVADO SUGAR OR BROWN SUGAR
60 ML (2 FL OZ/¼ CUP) COCONUT OIL
1 TEASPOON VANILLA BEAN PASTE
PINCH OF SALT

Grease and line a 20 cm (8 in) square baking tin with baking paper, leaving some overhanging on each side.

Put the oats, nuts, desiccated coconut and cherries in a large mixing bowl.

Combine the honey, sugar, coconut oil, vanilla and salt in a small saucepan over medium heat and cook until the mixture begins to bubble at the edges. Pour the honey mixture into the dry ingredients in the bowl and stir well until everything is coated.

Dump the mixture into the lined tin and press it down into the edges (I find the easiest way to do this is with slightly wet hands). Keep pressing the mixture very firmly for longer than you think is necessary – this is what will stop it from falling apart. Put the tin in the refrigerator to set for at least an hour.

When the mixture is totally chilled, remove it from the tin using the overhanging baking paper to lift it out. Slice into 10 bars.

Makes 10 bars

## BROWN RICE PUDDING WITH ROASTED STRAWBERRIES

*EXCUSE ME WHILE I GET ON DOWN TO COMFORT-FOOD TOWN. THE MAGIC OF THIS BROWN RICE PUDDING IS THAT IT SOOTHES AND SALVES YOUR ILLS IN THE WAY THAT ONLY CARBS CAN, AND YET IT FEELS HEALTHY AND VIRTUOUS AT THE SAME TIME. I DON'T THINK COMFORT-EATING IS SOMETHING TO FEEL BAD ABOUT. IN FACT, I THINK OF ALL FOOD AS COMFORT FOOD. BUT IT'S A RARE AND BEAUTIFUL THING WHEN A DISH IS SO NURSERY-LEVEL SOOTHING, AND YET FULL OF FIBRE AND FRUIT AT THE SAME TIME. LET'S WRAP OURSELVES IN BLANKETS AND EAT THIS FOR BREAKFAST, PLEASE.*

*BROWN RICE PUDDING*
500 ML (17 FL OZ/2 CUPS) ALMOND MILK (UNSWEETENED)
500 ML (17 FL OZ/2 CUPS) MILK
1 LITRE (34 FL OZ/4 CUPS) WATER
200 G (7 OZ/1 CUP) BROWN RICE
2 TABLESPOONS CASTER (SUPERFINE) SUGAR
2 TABLESPOONS BROWN SUGAR
2 TEASPOONS VANILLA BEAN PASTE
PINCH OF SALT

*ROASTED STRAWBERRIES*
500 G (1 LB 2 OZ/3⅓ CUPS) STRAWBERRIES, WASHED AND HULLED
2 TABLESPOONS CASTER (SUPERFINE) SUGAR
FLAKED ALMONDS, TO SERVE (OPTIONAL)

Put all the ingredients for the brown rice pudding in a large saucepan over medium heat and stir to combine. Bring to the boil, reduce the heat to low and simmer, stirring occasionally, for about an hour, or until the mixture thickens and the rice is cooked through. The rice will look like a soupy mess for the longest time, but it will come together at the end. It's a labour of love.

Preheat the oven to 200°C (400°F).

While the rice is cooking, slice the strawberries in half and toss them in a shallow roasting dish with the sugar. Leave them to macerate for at least 10 minutes.

Roast the berries for 10 minutes.

Serve the rice pudding in bowls with plenty of the roasted strawberries and some flaked almonds, if using.

Serves 4

# RASPBERRY COCONUT YOGHURT POPS

*SWIRLS GET THE GIRLS. I JUST INVENTED THAT SAYING. BECAUSE I CAN'T SPEAK FOR EVERYONE, I'M GOING TO DOWNGRADE IT TO SWIRLS GET THIS GIRL, BECAUSE I CANNOT RESIST A SWIRL, A RIPPLE OR A STRIATION OF ANY KIND. SO EVEN THOUGH THESE POPS ARE NOT AS INDULGENT AS, SAY, MY BLACKBERRY TRES LECHES CAKE (PAGE 110), WHICH ALSO FEATURES A RIPPLE, THEY STILL FEEL LIKE AN ABSOLUTE TREAT WHEN YOU PULL THEM OUT OF THE FREEZER. THE CREAMY COCONUT YOGHURT, TANGY LIME AND SWEET RASPBERRIES ARE PERFECT TOGETHER AND THESE POPSICLES WILL ONLY TAKE YOU 5-10 MINUTES TO MAKE. SO WHAT'S THE HOLD-UP?*

150 G (5½ OZ/1 CUP) FROZEN RASPBERRIES, DEFROSTED
½ LIME
60 G (2 OZ/½ CUP) ICING (CONFECTIONERS') SUGAR
375 G (13 OZ/1½ CUPS) COCONUT YOGHURT
1 TEASPOON VANILLA BEAN PASTE

Put the raspberries in a food processor or blender. Squeeze in the lime juice. Add half the sugar and blitz everything to a purée. I like to pass the purée through a sieve to remove the seeds, but it's up to you.

Put the coconut yoghurt, the rest of the sugar and the vanilla bean paste in a separate small bowl and stir together.

Layer the yoghurt and raspberry mixtures into popsicle moulds and place in the freezer to chill. After about 30 minutes, pop in your popsicle sticks and leave for another 4 hours at least to freeze solid.

To remove the popsicles from the moulds, you may need to dip your moulds into warm water for 10–15 seconds.

Makes 500 ml (17 fl oz/2 cups) mixture (see tip opposite)

**TIP** The number of popsicles this will make depends on the size of your moulds. To see how much you'll need, fill your moulds with water, then tip the water into a measuring pitcher. This recipe makes 500 ml (17 fl oz/2 cups) mixture, so if you need more, just scale everything up.

THIS RECIPE IS FOR MY DAD AND MY SISTER AND ALL THE OTHER COELIACS OUT THERE IN THE WIDE WORLD. THESE CUPCAKES ARE THE BOMB.COM. THEY ARE BUTTERY, LIGHT IN TEXTURE AND SCENTED WITH VANILLA. THEY COME TOGETHER JUST AS SIMPLY AND EASILY AS REGULAR CUPCAKES, AND THERE IS ONLY ONE WEIRD-SOUNDING INGREDIENT (XANTHAN GUM – WHICH YOU CAN FIND AT ANY HEALTH FOOD STORE AND A LOT OF SUPERMARKETS). GIVE THESE TO YOUR FRIENDS, WHETHER THEY EAT GLUTEN OR NOT, AND WATCH EACH AND EVERY ONE OF THEM ENJOY A FLIPPING DELICIOUS CUPCAKE. THEY WILL NEVER KNOW THAT THESE ARE GLUTEN-FREE. THEY'RE JUST THAT GOOD.

CUPCAKES
55 G (2 OZ/½ CUP) BESAN (CHICKPEA FLOUR)
45 G (1½ OZ/¼ CUP) WHITE RICE FLOUR
30 G (1 OZ/¼ CUP) CORNFLOUR (CORNSTARCH)
½ TEASPOON XANTHAN GUM
1½ TEASPOONS BAKING POWDER
115 G (4 OZ/½ CUP) CASTER (SUPERFINE) SUGAR
125 G (4½ OZ) BUTTER, SOFTENED
2 EGGS
2 TABLESPOONS MILK
2 TEASPOONS VANILLA BEAN PASTE

BUTTERCREAM
150 G (5½ OZ) BUTTER, SOFTENED
335 G (12 OZ/2⅔ CUPS) ICING (CONFECTIONERS') SUGAR
1 TEASPOON VANILLA BEAN PASTE
2 TABLESPOONS MILK

TO DECORATE
NATURAL FOOD COLOURING (OPTIONAL)
SPRINKLES (OPTIONAL)

Preheat the oven to 180°C (350°F) and line a 12-hole muffin tin with paper cases.

To make the cupcakes, put all the dry ingredients and the butter in a bowl and beat with electric beaters (or use a stand mixer with the paddle attachment) until the mixture looks like breadcrumbs. Continue beating on medium speed and add the eggs one at a time. Turn the speed up to high and beat just until combined. Add the milk and vanilla and beat briefly until smooth and combined. Be careful not to over-mix.

Divide the mixture evenly between the paper cases and bake for 18–20 minutes, or until golden brown and the cakes spring back when touched lightly. Put the cakes on a wire rack and leave to cool completely before icing.

To make the buttercream, beat the butter until soft. Add half the icing sugar and beat until smooth. Add the remaining icing sugar, beat until smooth, then add the vanilla and milk and beat on high speed until very pale and fluffy – add the food colouring now, if using. Spread a thick layer of buttercream onto each of the cooled cakes with a palette knife or spatula, creating peaks and swirls as you go. Decorate with sprinkles, if desired.

Makes 12

# PINEAPPLE AND MELON CARPACCIO WITH MOJITO SUGAR

AUSTRALIA DAY IS 26 JANUARY, WHICH IS ALSO MY SISTER'S BIRTHDAY. AT ONE MEMORABLE CELEBRATION THERE WAS A VODKA-FILLED WATERMELON, OF WHICH I ATE WAAAAAY TOO MUCH. I DO NOT RECOMMEND DOING THAT. BUT THE JUICY FRUIT AND BOOZE COMBINATION WAS UNDENIABLY DELICIOUS AND PERFECT FOR A HOT DAY. THIS IS MY SLIGHTLY FANCIER TAKE ON THAT IDEA - PINEAPPLE, ROCKMELON (CANTALOUPE/NETTED MELON) AND WATERMELON, SERVED WITH A MOJITO-FLAVOURED SUGAR. WHETHER OR NOT YOU WANT TO POUR A LITTLE WHITE RUM OVER THE FRUIT IS ENTIRELY UP TO YOU. BUT DON'T SAY I DIDN'T WARN YOU.

1 SMALL PINEAPPLE
$1/2$ ROCKMELON (CANTALOUPE/NETTED MELON)
$1/4$ WATERMELON

MOJITO SUGAR
110 G (4 OZ/$1/2$ CUP) RAW (DEMERARA) SUGAR
1 SMALL BUNCH MINT
GRATED ZEST OF 1 LIME
WHITE RUM, TO SERVE (OPTIONAL)

Peel the pineapple and slice it into quarters lengthways. Lay each piece on its side and carefully cut away the core. Slice the pieces into long, thin strips about 5 mm (¼ in) thick.

Seed the rockmelon and slice into thin strips, a similar size to the pineapple.

Do the same for the watermelon.

To make the mojito sugar, you have options. Either put the sugar, mint and lime zest in a blender or food processor and pulse until everything is green and incorporated, or use a mortar and pestle and bash away at the ingredients until the mint and zest are absorbed into the sugar.

To serve, place the pineapple and melon pieces decoratively on a large platter and sprinkle lightly with a few teaspoons of the mojito sugar. Serve the remaining sugar on the side for people to add as they please. If you're feeling saucy, you can drizzle a little rum over the fruit before adding the sugar.

Serves 6

**TIP** If you have any left-over sugar, spread it out on a lined baking tray and leave it in a dry, cool place overnight. The sugar will dry out, and can then be broken up and stored for a week or so in an airtight container. Do make sure to let it dry completely, though, or it might go mouldy. It makes a fantastic addition to cocktails, to rim your glasses with, or as an unusual coating for doughnuts.

*BASICALLY, A HUGE PLATE OF FRESH PEACHES WITH A PILE OF LUMINESCENT RASPBERRY GRANITA MOUNDED ON TOP. I LIKE TO THINK OF THIS AS PEACH MELBA FOR THE HOTTEST DAY OF THE YEAR. THE BLUSHING, SUNSET-ORANGE PEACHES – AS RIPE AS YOU CAN GET THEM – CONTRAST BEAUTIFULLY WITH THE LUDICROUSLY RUBY-RED GRANITA. IT'S IMPOSSIBLE TO BE SAD WITH FOOD THIS BEAUTIFUL IN FRONT OF YOU. OH, AND IT'S VEGAN.*

115 G (4 OZ/$\frac{1}{2}$ CUP) CASTER (SUPERFINE) SUGAR
185 G (6$\frac{1}{2}$ OZ/1$\frac{1}{2}$ CUPS) FRESH RASPBERRIES OR 185 G (6$\frac{1}{2}$ OZ/1$\frac{1}{4}$ CUPS) FROZEN RASPBERRIES
4 PEACHES

Put the sugar and 250 ml (8$\frac{1}{2}$ fl oz/1 cup) water in a small saucepan and stir over low heat until the sugar dissolves. Bring the mixture to the boil, then turn off the heat and add the raspberries. If you're using frozen raspberries, let them sit in the mixture until defrosted.

Pour the mixture through a sieve into a small metal baking tray, pushing through as much of the raspberry pulp as you can, and leaving the seeds behind. Give the mix a stir, then put it in the freezer. After an hour, stir the mixture with a fork, breaking up any ice crystals and bringing the edges into the middle. Put it back in the freezer and leave to set completely.

To serve, either peel the peaches by cutting a cross into the base of each one, pouring over some hot water and then rinsing and peeling off the skins, or just leave the skin on. Either way, cut the peaches into quarters (removing the stones) and arrange them on a platter. Using a fork, scrape up the granita into a pile of snowy crystals, then pile it onto the peaches and serve straight away.

Serves 4–6

**TIP** It's best to keep the platter and the peaches as cold as possible, because the granita will start melting pretty quickly. In fact, it's best to cut the peaches, plate them up and then refrigerate the whole platter early so all you have to do is pile on the granita and serve ASAP when you want to eat.

# POACHED PEARS WITH COCONUT CHOCOLATE SAUCE

POACHED PEARS AND CHOCOLATE SAUCE IS A CLASSIC FRENCH DESSERT CALLED POIRES BELLE HÉLÈNE. THIS IS MY UPDATED VERSION, WHICH USES A SIMPLE HONEY SYRUP TO POACH THE PEARS AND REPLACES THE CREAM IN THE SAUCE WITH COCONUT MILK. WHAT YOU END UP WITH NOT ONLY SKIPS THE REFINED SUGAR AND DAIRY, BUT IT IS ALSO MORE FRAGRANT, A LITTLE LIGHTER AND HAS MORE DEPTH OF FLAVOUR THAN THE ORIGINAL. I LOVE HOW THIS DESSERT IS SOMEHOW BOTH COMFORTING AND CHIC AT THE SAME TIME.

4 PEARS (WILLIAMS PEARS ARE GREAT, BUT ANY WILL WORK)
80 ML (2½ FL OZ/⅓ CUP) HONEY
1 VANILLA BEAN, SPLIT LENGTHWAYS AND SEEDS SCRAPED, POD RESERVED

COCONUT CHOCOLATE SAUCE
100 G (3½ OZ) DARK CHOCOLATE (70% COCOA SOLIDS)
125 ML (4 FL OZ/½ CUP) COCONUT MILK

Peel the pears, slice them in half lengthways and remove the cores. (I find it easiest to gouge them out with a teaspoon. A melon baller would be perfect, but who owns a melon baller?)

Put the pears in a deep, wide saucepan in which they fit snugly, then add enough water to cover – about 750 ml (25½ fl oz/3 cups). Add the honey, vanilla pod and seeds. Bring to the boil over medium heat, then reduce the heat to low and simmer until the pears are tender – anywhere from 5 to 20 minutes depending on their ripeness.

Once the pears are done, you can either serve them hot or leave them to cool and chill them overnight in their syrup.

To make the coconut chocolate sauce, break up the chocolate and put it in a small saucepan with the coconut milk. Melt gently over low heat, stirring, until it comes together in a glossy black sauce.

Serve the pears, warm or cold, drizzled with as much of the chocolate sauce as you like! This is also amazing with ice cream.

Serves 4

# CHEWY COCOA DATE FUDGE

*IF YOU ARE A FAN OF CHOCOLATE, PLEASE MEET YOUR NEW BEST FRIEND. I KNOW THIS MIGHT SEEM LIKE FAUX-FOOD - DATES AND COCOA POWDER PRETENDING TO BE BROWNIES OR SOMETHING. BUT IT'S NOT, I SWEAR. IT JUST TASTES GOOD. THE CARAMEL TASTE AND TEXTURE OF THE DATES WITH THE SAVOURY PECANS, THE BITTER COCOA AND SMOKY MAPLE SYRUP; ALL THESE THINGS COMBINE TO MAKE SOMETHING SO MUCH GREATER THAN THE SUM OF ITS PARTS. IT'S LIKE THE CARTOON CHARACTERS, EARTH, FIRE, WIND, WATER, HEART - THEIR POWERS COMBINE TO SUMMON CAPTAIN PLANET! BUT IN THIS CASE, YOU DON'T GET AN ICE-BLUE SUPER HERO, YOU GET FUDGE.*

300 G (10½ OZ/1⅔ CUPS) PITTED DATES (PITTED MEDJOOL DATES ARE GREAT, BUT REGULAR DATES WORK PERFECTLY)
200 G (7 OZ/2 CUPS) PECANS
2 TABLESPOONS UNSWEETENED (DUTCH) COCOA POWDER
2-4 TABLESPOONS MAPLE SYRUP
½ TEASPOON SEA SALT FLAKES

Line a 20 cm (8 in) square baking dish with baking paper.

Put the dates and pecans in the bowl of a food processor and process until the mixture begins to look like breadcrumbs. Stop the processor and add the cocoa, as well as 2 tablespoons of the maple syrup and the sea salt. Process again until the mixture changes colour and begins to clump together. Carefully taste a small amount. If you would like it to be sweeter, you can add the rest of the maple syrup. Give the mixture a final pulse.

Pour the mixture into the lined dish and press it in. Place in the refrigerator for 2–3 hours to firm up. Slice into small squares and eat!

Makes 20 small squares

**TIP** This mixture can also be rolled into 2 teaspoon-sized balls and tossed in cocoa powder to make a completely delicious raw truffle.

I AM A MAJOR BELIEVER IN THE FOOD-AS-MEDICINE PHILOSOPHY. WHEN YOU LOVE TO EAT AS MUCH AS I DO, IT'S IMPOSSIBLE TO IGNORE THE FACT THAT WHAT YOU EAT DIRECTLY AFFECTS HOW YOU FEEL. SOMETIMES IT'S PHYSIOLOGICAL AND SOMETIMES IT'S PSYCHOLOGICAL, BUT WHO CARES? WHEN I'M UNDER THE WEATHER AND IN FULL SELF-PITY MODE OVER THE FLU, THE FLU SHOT IS WHAT I WANT – SOMETHING WARM TO HUNCH OVER, THAT'S CRAMMED FULL OF INGREDIENTS TO ALLEVIATE MY SYMPTOMS. WATERMELON AND LIME JUICE IS RIDICULOUSLY REFRESHING AND PERFECT FOR HOT-WEATHER DAYS. A CITRUS AND POMEGRANATE SUNRISE IS WHAT I WANT TO DRINK EVERY MORNING. AND THE DATE SHAKE MANAGES TO BE THICK, CARAMELLY, SWEET AND LUXURIOUS WITH ONLY THE POWER OF DATES?! FOOD IS MAGIC. THAT'S THE TRUTH.

# THE FLU SHOT

JUICE OF 1/2 ORANGE
2 COIN-SIZED SLICES FRESH GINGER
2 SLICES LEMON
HONEY TO TASTE
PINCH OF GROUND TURMERIC (OPTIONAL)
125 ML (4 FL OZ/1/2 CUP) WATER

Put all the ingredients in a small saucepan over low heat. Bring to a simmer, turn off the heat and decant into a mug. Sip and feel better.

Serves 1

# WATERMELON AND LIME JUICE

1/4 LARGE WATERMELON, CHOPPED AND SEEDED
3 LIMES
ICE CUBES
MINT LEAVES (OPTIONAL)

Blend or process the watermelon until it is a slush. Pass the slush through a fine sieve and press with a spoon to get every last drop of juice through. Discard the flesh and any seeds left in the sieve. Squeeze in the juice of as many limes as you like (I like 3). Serve with lots of ice and a few leaves of mint in your glass, if desired.

Serves 2–4

# CITRUS AND POMEGRANATE SUNRISE

2 ORANGES
2 MANDARINS OR CLEMENTINES
1/2 LEMON
POMEGRANATE JUICE

Use a juicer or citrus press to juice the oranges and mandarins. Squeeze in the lemon juice. Divide between two glasses, top up with pomegranate juice and serve.

Serves 2

# DATE SHAKE

4 MEDJOOL DATES, PITTED
250 ML (8½ FL OZ/1 CUP) LOW-FAT MILK OR ALMOND MILK
1 TEASPOON VANILLA BEAN PASTE
135 G (5 OZ/1 CUP) ICE CUBES

Put the dates and about a third of the milk in a blender and process until the dates are puréed. Add the remaining milk, the vanilla and ice and blend again. Serve while still frosty cold.

Serves 2

# MIDNIGHT SNACKS

The first rule of midnight snacks is, you don't talk about midnight snacks. And that's the second rule as well. So I'm really going out on a limb to share these with you. That should demonstrate how important the art of the midnight snack is to me. In fact, I would make a great vampire, because I am more than happy to do all my feasting in the dead of night.

Like a vampire, you don't want to leave any evidence behind when you're midnight snackin'. The whole point of this operation is that only the people involved have any knowledge that it occurred, and even they might wake up thinking it was all just a glorious dream.

Midnight snacks are for after everyone else has left the party, and it's only you and your closest friends and confidants left. They're what you make when insomnia strikes and, instead of tossing and turning, you choose to embrace the dark of night and throw caution to the wind. They're completely unnecessary, and that's what makes them so fun.

There should be an element of Alice in Wonderland in every midnight meal – a stack of pancakes swelled to gigantic proportions (page 98), a savoury-looking jaffle filled with molten chocolate brownie (page 92), or a giant crispy cube of buttery toast, overflowing with ice cream, berries and maple syrup (page 100).

This chapter is about straight-up rule-breaking. If you're a three-meals-a-day stickler, then I'm afraid this just won't be for you. But if you're up for a little carpe diem-ing in the kitchen (or carpe noctem-ing, technically), then please follow me. Prepare yourself to fall down the rabbit hole, climb up the Faraway Tree, and have a tea party on the ceiling. Just don't forget rule number one.

# FILTHY CHEAT'S JAM DOUGHNUT

*THIS RECIPE IS NO JOKE. IT IS NOT KIDDING AROUND. IT'S GO TIME. THERE IS NO BETTER PLACE TO START THE MIDNIGHT SNACKS CHAPTER THAN HERE, BECAUSE IT SHOWS HOW SERIOUS I AM ABOUT THIS CATEGORY OF FOODS. THIS FILTHY CHEAT'S JAM DOUGHNUT IS SO DEADLY DELICIOUS, IT CAN ONLY BE CONSUMED IN THE DEAD OF NIGHT. GOD SPEED TO YOU, GOOD LUCK AND DON'T FORGET TO BE SUPER-CAREFUL WHILE YOU DEEP-FRY.*

4 X 1 CM (½ IN) SLICES BRIOCHE
4 TEASPOONS JAM OF YOUR CHOICE (RASPBERRY FOR ME)
CASTER (SUPERFINE) SUGAR, TO COAT
GRAPESEED OR CANOLA OIL FOR DEEP-FRYING

*BATTER*
2 EGGS
50 G (1¾ OZ/⅓ CUP) PLAIN (ALL-PURPOSE) FLOUR
80 ML (2½ FL OZ/⅓ CUP) MILK

First, make the batter by whisking the eggs in a small bowl, then whisk in the flour and finally the milk. You should have a batter the texture of pouring (single/light) cream, with maybe a couple of small lumps here and there.

Next, cut the crusts off your brioche slices (you can cut them into a circle shape if you like). Take 2 of the slices and dollop half the jam into the centre of each, then top with the remaining pieces of brioche, lightly pressing around the edges so the jam doesn't splodge out.

Put the caster sugar on a plate.

Pour about 5 cm (2 in) of oil into a deep saucepan over low heat, and bring up to 170°C (340°F), or until a cube of bread turns brown in 20 seconds.

Working quickly, take a brioche sandwich and dip it in the batter, making sure that the whole sandwich is sealed in batter. Carefully lower the sandwich into the oil, and cook for about 30 seconds to a minute per side, or until golden brown. Remove the sandwich with a slotted spoon, and let the oil drain into the pan, before tossing it in the caster sugar and turning it around carefully to coat. Repeat with the remaining sandwich, then try not to burn your mouth on the mega-hot jam!

Serves 2

# WHIPPED CHEESECAKE WITH HONEY-SOAKED GREEK PASTRY

*THIS IS A NO-BAKE WHIPPED CHEESECAKE, SERVED ON A BASE OF CRUNCHY PASTRY. IT'S SIMPLE. ALL THE ELEMENTS CAN BE MADE AHEAD AND, BECAUSE EACH ONE IS PLATED INDIVIDUALLY, THERE IS A MAJOR ELEGANCE TO THIS DESSERT. IT'S PERFECT FOR THOSE TIMES WHEN YOU WANT YOUR MIDNIGHT SNACK TO BE IRRESISTIBLY TEXTURAL AND MOREISH, BUT ALSO REFINED.*

*WHIPPED CHEESECAKE*
250 G (9 OZ/1 CUP) CREAM CHEESE, AT ROOM TEMPERATURE
55 G (2 OZ/¼ CUP) CASTER (SUPERFINE) SUGAR
GRATED ZEST OF 1 LEMON
125 ML (4 FL OZ/½ CUP) THICKENED (WHIPPING) CREAM (35% FAT)

*PASTRY NESTS*
300 G (10½ OZ) KATAIFI PASTRY (SEE TIP OPPOSITE)
50 G (1¾ OZ) BUTTER
125 ML (4 FL OZ/½ CUP) HONEY

*BLUEBERRIES*
125 G (4½ OZ) BLUEBERRIES
1 TABLESPOON CASTER (SUPERFINE) SUGAR
1 TABLESPOON WATER

*TO SERVE*
CRUSHED PISTACHIO NUTS

For the cheesecake, put the cream cheese, sugar and lemon zest in a mixing bowl and beat until smooth and combined.

Whip the cream to stiff peaks and fold through the cream cheese. Put in the refrigerator to set for at least 2 hours.

For the pastry nests, preheat the oven to 180°C (350°F) and line a baking tray with baking paper.

Take a sixth of the pastry and wrap it around your fingers as though you're making a coil of rope, then slide it off your hand and onto the baking tray, forming a nest about the size of a drink coaster. Repeat with the rest of the pastry. Bake for 10–15 minutes or until golden brown.

Meanwhile, melt the butter and honey together in a small saucepan over low heat.

When the pastry nests are baked, drizzle them liberally with the honey–butter mixture. Set aside to cool completely.

For the blueberries, put all the ingredients in a small saucepan over medium heat and cook just until the blueberries start to break down. Set aside and allow to cool.

To serve, dollop a generous amount of the cheesecake on a pastry nest and top with a spoonful of the blueberries and some crushed pistachio nuts.

Serves 6

**TIP** Kataifi pastry is a traditional Greek ingredient, kind of like long, thin shreds of filo pastry.

DIPPED CONES MAKE AN AWESOME MIDNIGHT SNACK FOR A MILLION SUPER-OBVIOUS REASONS. HOW ELSE CAN I EXPLAIN ALL MY PYJAMA-CLAD, LATE-NIGHT ICE CREAM RUNS TO THE 7/11? BUT THOSE FACTORY-MADE ICE CREAMS ARE PRETTY BOGUS – THE ICE CREAM DOESN'T REALLY MELT, AND THE CHOCOLATE LAYER IS THIN AND WEIRD. A HOMEMADE CONE IS BETTER IN EVERY WAY, AND THEY'RE SO FUN TO MAKE. YOU CAN EASILY DO THIS WITH ANY STORE-BOUGHT ICE CREAM BUT, IF YOU'VE COME THIS FAR, WHY NOT MAKE YOUR OWN? MY THREE FAVOURITE ICE CREAM RECIPES ARE ON PAGES 88, 90 AND 96. THE BASIC TECHNIQUE I USE COMES FROM JENI'S SPLENDID ICE CREAMS AT HOME, AN AWESOME BOOK BY JENI BRITTON BAUER, WHICH IS FULL OF OTHER INCREDIBLE FLAVOURS. NOW GET DIPPIN'!

1 LITRE (34 FL OZ/4 CUPS) ICE CREAM
8 WAFFLE CONES
TOPPINGS TO SPRINKLE (OPTIONAL)

CHOCOLATE SAUCE
200 G (7 OZ) DARK CHOCOLATE (70% COCOA SOLIDS)
60 ML (2 FL OZ/¼ CUP) COCONUT OIL

First, take your ice cream and put a healthy amount into each cone. You want the ice cream to be firmly packed in there, but be careful not to crack the cones.

Sit the cones in a cup or a pitcher (or a couple of them), and put them in the freezer for at least an hour.

Melt the chocolate and coconut oil together in a small bowl in the microwave. I do this on High (100%) for 20 seconds at a time, stirring after each burst, but you could also do it in a bowl over a saucepan of simmering water, making sure the base of the bowl isn't touching the water.

Pour the melted mixture into a nice, deep container that is just wide enough to fit your cones. A smallish drinking glass or jam jar is pretty perfect. Working quickly, dip one cone at a time in the chocolate mixture, letting any excess drip away. Quickly sprinkle on any toppings, if using, and then put the cones back in the freezer to set for about an hour.

Makes 8

*Zangy passionfruit is one of my favourite fruits, and it marries so well with chocolate. What I love about this cone is that it takes a kid's flavour – s'mores – and somehow manages to be sophisticated, grown-up and intriguing, purely through the addition of passionfruit. These cones are a game-changer. PS – don't be afraid to really singe those marshmallows!*

PASSIONFRUIT ICE CREAM
500 ML (17 FL OZ/2 CUPS) FULL-CREAM (WHOLE) MILK
20G (¾ OZ) CORNFLOUR (CORNSTARCH)
1½ TABLESPOONS CREAM CHEESE, AT ROOM TEMPERATURE
PINCH OF SALT
310 ML (10½ FL OZ/1¼ CUPS) THICKENED (WHIPPING) CREAM (35% FAT)
145 G (5 OZ/⅔ CUP) CASTER (SUPERFINE) SUGAR
2 TABLESPOONS LIQUID GLUCOSE (OR CORN SYRUP)
60 G (2 OZ/⅔ CUP) VANILLA (OR PASSIONFRUIT) MARSHMALLOWS
125 ML (4 FL OZ/½ CUP) PASSIONFRUIT PURÉE, WITH SOME SEEDS

TO SERVE
8 WAFFLE CONES
CHOCOLATE SAUCE (PAGE 86)

Put 2 tablespoons of the milk in a small bowl with the cornflour and stir together well.

Put the cream cheese in a large mixing bowl with the salt and whisk until smooth.

Put the remaining milk in a saucepan over high heat, with the cream, sugar and glucose and bring to the boil. Boil for 4 minutes, then remove from the heat and whisk in the cornflour mixture. Return to the heat and cook, stirring, for about 1 minute, or until thickened.

Pour the ice cream mixture, bit by bit, into the bowl with the cream cheese, whisking continuously to make sure there are no lumps.

Chill the ice cream mixture completely in the refrigerator (I usually leave it overnight).

When you're ready to churn the ice cream, spread the marshmallows out on a foil-lined baking tray and toast and slightly char them with either a kitchen blowtorch or under a grill (broiler) at high heat.

Stir the passionfruit purée and seeds into the ice cream base. Churn in your ice cream maker, according to the manufacturer's instructions. Pack into a freezer-safe container, scraping up and layering in the marshmallows as you go. Cover with baking paper and freeze.
Follow the instructions on page 86 to dip and finish the cones.

Makes 8

**TIP** If you have never heard of s'mores, then you've obviously never seen *The Sandlot*, and you're killing me, Smalls. It's a toasted marshmallow, with some milk chocolate sandwiched between two crisp cookies.

If the idea of this recipe makes you raise an eyebrow or wrinkle your nose, or you just don't like pretzels, you should still make it. This is, without a doubt, my favourite flavour of ice cream. It is indescribably, transcendently good. And, when it's rippled with salty caramel, packed into a cone, dipped in chocolate and sprinkled with crushed pretzels? It's unbeatable! If this food writer thing doesn't work out, I'm just going to go into business selling pretzel cones. I'll be a millionaire.

PRETZEL ICE CREAM
300 G (10½ OZ/3 CUPS) PRETZELS, PLUS EXTRA FOR SPRINKLING
500 ML (17 FL OZ/2 CUPS) FULL-CREAM (WHOLE) MILK
20 G (¾ OZ) CORNFLOUR (CORNSTARCH)
1½ TABLESPOONS CREAM CHEESE, AT ROOM TEMPERATURE
310 ML (10½ FL OZ/1¼ CUPS) THICKENED (WHIPPING) CREAM (35% FAT)
145 G (5 OZ/⅔ CUP) CASTER (SUPERFINE) SUGAR
2 TABLESPOONS LIQUID GLUCOSE OR CORN SYRUP
½ BATCH SALTED CARAMEL (PAGE 9)

TO SERVE
8 WAFFLE CONES
CHOCOLATE SAUCE (PAGE 86)

Preheat the oven to 170°C (340°F) and line a baking tray with baking paper.

Crush the pretzels lightly in your hands roughly into quarters and spread them out on the lined baking tray. Bake for 10–15 minutes or until your kitchen smells like pretzels, and the pretzels themselves are darkened.

Put the pretzels in a mixing bowl and pour over the milk. Leave to steep, stirring occasionally, for about 10 minutes. The milk will take on a light beige colour.

Remove about 2 tablespoons of the steeped milk, and put it in a small bowl with the cornstarch. Stir together well. Strain the remaining milk into a saucepan, and discard the soaked pretzels. You should have about 375 ml (12½ fl oz/1½ cups) pretzel-flavoured milk.

Clean out the bowl and put the cream cheese in it, whisking until smooth.

Add the cream, sugar and glucose to the pretzel milk in the saucepan, and bring to the boil over high heat. Boil for 4 minutes, then remove from the heat and whisk in the cornflour mixture. Return to the heat and cook, stirring, for about 1 minute or until thickened.

Pour the hot cream mixture, bit by bit, into the cream cheese, whisking continuously to make sure there are no lumps.

Chill the ice cream mixture completely in the refrigerator (I usually leave it overnight).

Churn in your ice cream maker, according to the manufacturer's instructions. Pack into a freezer-safe container, rippling through the salted caramel as you go, then cover with baking paper and freeze. Follow the instructions on page 86 to dip and finish the cones, sprinkling over or pressing in the extra pretzels as you go.

Makes 8

# MOLTEN BROWNIE JAFFLE

*No other recipe in this book makes me feel like an evil dessert genius more than this one. I know it's not the biggest or the flashiest recipe in the book, but it is the most ridiculous, 'you-gotta-be-kidding-me' example of my insanity. It's exactly what it says it is – a molten-centred brownie … in a jaffle. Hallelujah.*

75 G (2¾ OZ) BUTTER, PLUS EXTRA IF NECESSARY
75 G (2¾ OZ) DARK CHOCOLATE (70% COCOA SOLIDS)
55 G (2 OZ/¼ CUP) CASTER (SUPERFINE) SUGAR
1 EGG
2 TABLESPOONS PLAIN (ALL-PURPOSE) FLOUR
8 SLICES WHITE BREAD
ICING (CONFECTIONERS') SUGAR

*FILLINGS*
PEANUT BUTTER
CRUSHED OR CHOPPED NUTS
SALTED CARAMEL (PAGE 9)
ANYTHING ELSE YOU WANT!

Melt the butter and chocolate together in a heat-safe bowl in the microwave in 20-second bursts on High (100%), stirring well after each burst.

When the chocolate and butter are melted, stir in the sugar, followed by the egg and finally the flour. Beat the mixture with a wooden spoon until it comes together in a smooth, silky batter. Put the batter in the refrigerator for 20 minutes to cool down.

Preheat the jaffle maker.

Butter the bread on one side and sift over a fine layer of icing sugar. On the non-buttered side of 4 of the slices of bread, pile on a quarter of the filling, plus a few blobs or sprinkles of anything else you might like to add. Top the fillings with the other pieces of bread, butter-side out.

Place carefully in your jaffle maker and cook until golden brown. Serve immediately, but beware – as with all jaffles, this thing is lava-hot on the inside.

Makes 4 jaffles

# DULCE DE LECHE CRÊPES

THIS RECIPE HAS A MIXED HERITAGE. DULCE DE LECHE IS SOUTH AMERICAN, THE TITLE IS A LITTLE BIT FRENCH AND THE CRÊPE RECIPE IS ACTUALLY SWEDISH. BUT ALL OF THAT IS PRETTY MUCH IMMATERIAL, BECAUSE THIS RECIPE TRANSCENDS ALL THOSE TIES TO BECOME SOMETHING THAT WILL BRING PEOPLE TOGETHER.

*CRÊPES*
3 EGGS
PINCH OF SALT
110 G (4 OZ/¾ CUP) PLAIN (ALL-PURPOSE) FLOUR
310 ML (10½ FL OZ/1¼ CUPS) MILK
BUTTER FOR GREASING

*SAUCE*
15 G (½ OZ) BUTTER
350 G (12½ OZ/1 CUP) DULCE DE LECHE (SEE TIP OPPOSITE)
125 ML (4 FL OZ/½ CUP) MILK
1 SHOT OF BRANDY (OR YOUR BOOZE OF CHOICE)
50 G (1¾ OZ/½ CUP) PECANS, CHOPPED
SEA SALT FLAKES

To make the crêpes, put the eggs and salt in a large mixing bowl and whisk to combine. Add the flour all in one go and whisk until there are no lumps. Continue whisking and slowly stream in the milk. You should have a smooth, thin batter.

Heat a 20 cm (8 in) frying pan (cast iron is great) over medium heat. Once the pan is hot, grease lightly with butter and then ladle in just under 60 ml (2 fl oz/¼ cup) of the batter. Immediately tilt and swirl the pan so the batter coats the base in a thin layer. Cook the crêpe just until the surface looks dry and set, then flip using a thin spatula or palette knife. The second side only needs a few seconds. Continue until all the batter is used, greasing the pan lightly every couple of crêpes. Once the crêpes are all cooked, cover them with foil to keep warm, while you make the sauce.

For the sauce, heat the butter in the same pan, and add the dulce de leche. Cook over low heat until the mixture is smooth, then slowly whisk in the milk and brandy. Bring to a bubble, then turn the heat down to the lowest possible setting.

Working one at a time, put a crêpe in the sauce, completely submerge it, fold it into quarters, then transfer to a serving plate. Continue until all the crêpes are done. Scatter over the pecans and a generous sprinkling of sea salt and serve.

Serves 4

# CHOCOLATE-HAZELNUT ICE CREAM IN BRIOCHE

*Thanks to Nigella Lawson, through two of her awesome books (Forever Summer and Nigellissima), I have learned that this is how they eat their ice cream in the South of Italy – stuffed into a brioche bun, like an ice cream burger. Chocolate-hazelnut spread is actually an Italian ingredient, based on the classic gianduja paste, which originated in Piemonte. In this glorious midnight-munch, the north and the south finally come together. I try to channel a Sophia Loren-type 1960s Italian babe whenever I eat these, with winged eye-liner and big hair. But I'm going to be honest, that's mostly in my imagination. The reality is much stickier.*

CHOCOLATE-HAZELNUT ICE CREAM
45 G (1½ OZ) CREAM CHEESE
PINCH OF SALT
190 G (6½ OZ) CASTER (SUPERFINE) SUGAR
60 G (2 OZ/½ CUP) UNSWEETENED (DUTCH) COCOA POWDER
310 G (11 OZ/1 CUP) CHOCOLATE-HAZELNUT SPREAD
500 ML (17 FL OZ/2 CUPS) FULL-CREAM (WHOLE) MILK
1½ TABLESPOONS CORNFLOUR (CORNSTARCH)
250 ML (8½ FL OZ/1 CUP) THICKENED (WHIPPING) CREAM (35% FAT)
2 TABLESPOONS LIQUID GLUCOSE (OR CORN SYRUP)

TO SERVE
UP TO 8 STORE-BOUGHT BRIOCHE BUNS, HALVED
CHOPPED HAZELNUTS

Put the cream cheese and salt in a large bowl.

In a small saucepan over medium-high heat, combine 125 ml (4 fl oz/½ cup) water, 75 g (2¾ oz) of the sugar and the cocoa, bring to the boil and cook for 30 seconds.

Whisk the hot cocoa mixture into the cream cheese slowly, bit by bit, making sure there are no lumps. Add the chocolate-hazelnut spread, stir everything well to combine, then set aside.

In a small bowl, stir together 2 tablespoons of the milk with the cornflour and set aside.

Put the remaining milk, the cream, remaining sugar and the glucose in a large saucepan and bring to the boil over high heat, letting it boil for 4 minutes.

Remove the pan from the heat, whisk in the cornflour mixture, then return the pan to the heat for a minute or until thickened slightly.

Stir the milk mixture into the chocolate-hazelnut mixture and put in the refrigerator to chill completely, for at least 6 hours or overnight.

Churn in an ice cream maker, according to the manufacturer's instructions. Pack into a freezer-safe container, cover with baking paper and store in the freezer.

To serve, put a scoop of ice cream in the bottom of a soft brioche bun, scatter over chopped hazelnuts, top with the other half of the brioche bun and devour.

Makes 1 litre (34 fl oz/4 cups) ice cream (enough to fill up to 8 buns)

# GIANT PANCAKE STACK

THIS IS MY ULTIMATE BUTTERMILK PANCAKE RECIPE – IT MAKES THE THICKEST, FLUFFIEST, MOST HEAVENLY PANCAKES YOU CAN IMAGINE. THEY'RE SO THICK THAT MY BOYFRIEND CALLS THEM FATTY CAKES, WHICH IS JUST ONE EXAMPLE OF HOW AWESOME HE IS. I HAVE THREE SUGGESTIONS FOR HOW YOU CAN AND SHOULD PIMP OUT THIS UNCLE BUCK-SIZED STACK OF PANCAKES:

1. STIR 125 G (4 1/2 OZ/1 CUP) CHOPPED PECANS INTO THE PANCAKE BATTER, DOUSE THE STACK WITH SALTED CARAMEL (PAGE 9) AND EAT WITH ICE CREAM.

2. MAKE A BATCH OF MAPLE-GLAZED BACON (PAGE 31) AND SERVE WITH EXTRA MAPLE SYRUP AND BUTTER.

3. COVER IN WHATEVER DELICIOUS NONSENSE HAPPENS TO BE IN YOUR REFRIGERATOR RIGHT NOW. I'M TALKING JAMS, NUTS, SYRUP, CHOCOLATE CHIPS, WHIPPED CREAM – ALL OF IT.

```
450 G (1 LB/3 CUPS) PLAIN (ALL-PURPOSE) FLOUR
1 1/2 TABLESPOONS BAKING POWDER
1 1/2 TEASPOONS BICARBONATE OF SODA (BAKING SODA)
45 G (1 1/2 OZ) CASTER (SUPERFINE) SUGAR
1 TEASPOON SALT
750 ML (25 1/2 FL OZ/3 CUPS) BUTTERMILK
3 EGGS
75 G (2 3/4 OZ) BUTTER, MELTED, PLUS EXTRA FOR THE PAN
ICE CREAM, TO SERVE
SPRINKLES TO GARNISH
```

Put the flour, baking powder, bicarbonate of soda, sugar and salt in a large mixing bowl. Make a well in the centre and add the remaining ingredients. Stir everything together until just combined – don't over-mix, a few lumps are desirable.

Put a large frying pan over medium heat. When the pan is hot, add a tiny amount of butter, about 1/2 teaspoon, then dollop in about 125 ml (4 fl oz/1/2 cup) of batter. Spread out to form a 15 cm (6 in) pancake and cook until the edges set and bubbles appear on the surface. Flip and cook for a further minute or so, and then slide onto a serving platter. Continue until all the batter is used up.

Serves 6–8

**TIP** This batter is legit. It's really easy to scale up and down. A third of this batch is the perfect amount for two – and how to make perfect pancakes for two is incredibly powerful knowledge!

# SHIBUYA TOAST

*I WISH I COULD TELL YOU A COOL STORY ABOUT THE HISTORY OF THIS RECIPE; BUT ALAS, I DON'T REALLY KNOW IT. ALL I KNOW IS THAT AFTER SEEING A FEW INSTAGRAMS, PLENTY OF TUMBLR POSTS AND ONE INSANE VIDEO, I HAD TO HAVE IT. THIS IS THE KIND OF THING THAT TAKES NO TIME TO MAKE (IT'S MOSTLY AN ASSEMBLY JOB), BUT IT LOOKS SO AWESOME AND IS SO MUNCHY AND CRUNCHY AND DELICIOUS, IT'S THE PERFECT THING TO PRESENT TO YOUR MATES AT MIDNIGHT. THEY WILL DESTROY IT.*

$1/3$ LOAF WHITE BAKERY BREAD
75 G (2¾ OZ) BUTTER, MELTED

*TO SERVE*
VANILLA ICE CREAM
FRESH BERRIES
WHIPPED CREAM
MAPLE SYRUP

Turn the loaf of bread on its end and, using a small serrated knife, slice a square about 1 cm (½ in) in from the edge of the loaf. Carefully scoop out the inside square of the loaf, trying not to squash it, leaving the crust of the loaf intact. Slice the inside of the loaf into large cubes.

Preheat the oven to 200°C (400°F) and line a baking tray with baking paper.

Heat about half the butter in a large frying pan over medium heat, and cook the bread cubes on all sides until golden brown and crisp. Put them on the baking tray.

Melt the remaining butter and brush it all over the crust of the loaf. Put the crust on the baking tray with the fried cubes and bake for 15 minutes or until crisp.

Pile the cubes into the shell, top with ice cream, berries and whipped cream, drizzle with maple syrup and serve.

Serves 2–4

# 'LIKE A FAT KID LOVES' MILKSHAKES

THIS IS IT, THE MIDNIGHT OF ALL MIDNIGHT SNACKS. I DON'T THINK THIS MILKSHAKE EVEN EXISTS IN DAYLIGHT HOURS. IT'S JUST SO DEVIANT THAT IT SIMPLY CANNOT BE TOUCHED BY THE SUN'S RAYS. I LOVE THIS MILKSHAKE, LIKE A FAT KID LOVES CAKE! THAT'S RIGHT - THIS IS A CAKE MILKSHAKE. AND I'LL TELL YOU WHEN YOU SHOULD DRINK THIS - ON THE THIRD DAY AFTER YOUR BIRTHDAY. WHEN YOUR SPARKLY NEW CLOTHES ARE DISHEVELLED AND DISCARDED, WHEN ALL THE WRAPPING PAPER IS THROWN AWAY AND YOUR BIRTHDAY CAKE IS JUST A CRUMBLING MOUND LEFT IN THE REFRIGERATOR, GROWING SLOWLY STALER. THIS MILKSHAKE DOES EXACTLY WHAT YOU SHOULD DO - TAKES SOME OF THAT CRUMBLING MOUND AND TURNS IT INTO SOMETHING EVEN BETTER THAN THE ORIGINAL. NOW THAT'S A HAPPY BIRTHDAY.

THIS IS MORE OF A FORMULA THAN A RECIPE. THE POINT IS, CAKE IN A MILKSHAKE IS INSANE. BUT THERE ARE A FEW RULES. FIRST, YOU NEED MORE CAKE THAN ICING. I LIKE TO TAKE A HEALTHY SLICE OF MY EPIC CANDY BAR LAYER CAKE (PAGE 130) AND THEN LOSE ONE OF THE LAYERS OF ICING BEFORE BLENDING. IF YOU'RE USING CUPCAKES, YOU NEED ABOUT ONE AND A HALF. MY FAVOURITE COMBO IS A MALTY CHOCOLATE CAKE WITH VANILLA ICE CREAM, FOR THAT COOKIES-AND-CREAM VIBE. BUT THIS IS YOUR PARTY, SO FEEL FREE TO USE WHATEVER CAKE/ICE CREAM COMBO YOU WANT!

1 PIECE OF BIRTHDAY CAKE
3 SCOOPS OF ICE CREAM
60–125 ML (2-4 FL OZ/¼-½ CUP) MILK
WHIPPED CREAM, TO SERVE
MARASCHINO CHERRY, TO SERVE

Throw the birthday cake, ice cream and 60 ml (2 fl oz/¼ cup) of the milk into a blender and whizz it up. Check the consistency – I like a thicker shake, but add the extra milk if you want it. Pour into your most old-fashioned milkshake glass and top with a dollop of whipped cream and a maraschino cherry.

Serves 1

# DROWNIE (BROWNIE AFFOGATO)

*I FIRST IMAGINED THIS RECIPE AS I WAS JUST FALLING ASLEEP MANY YEARS AGO, BUT THEN AFFOGATO' BOUT IT …*

*SORRY, THAT WAS TERRIBLE. I APOLOGISE. PLEASE DON'T HOLD THAT BAD PUN AGAINST THIS RECIPE, BECAUSE IT'S A WINNER. BROWNIE. ICE CREAM. COFFEE. BOOM – AMAZING. THE TRICK IS IN THE BROWNIE. IT HAS TO BE A REALLY CHOCOLATE-HEAVY, TRUFFLE-Y MIX, SO THAT IT MELTS SEDUCTIVELY UNDER THE HOT ESPRESSO. LADIES AND GENTLEMEN, THIS IS THAT BROWNIE.*

*BROWNIES*
150 G (5½ OZ) DARK CHOCOLATE (70% COCOA SOLIDS)
150 G (5½ OZ) BUTTER
145 G (5 OZ/⅔ CUP) CASTER (SUPERFINE) SUGAR
1 TABLESPOON UNSWEETENED (DUTCH) COCOA POWDER
2 EGGS
110 G (4 OZ/1 CUP) HAZELNUT MEAL

*TO SERVE*
1 SCOOP OF VANILLA ICE CREAM PER PERSON
1 SHOT OF ESPRESSO PER PERSON

To make the brownies, preheat the oven to 180°C (350°F) and line a 20 cm (8 in) square baking tin with baking paper.

Melt the chocolate and butter together in a saucepan over very low heat. When the chocolate is melted, remove the pan from the heat and add the sugar, cocoa and eggs. Stir everything together until well combined, and finally stir in the hazelnut meal. You should have a grainy, glossy mixture – if it looks separated, beat with a wooden spoon until it comes together.

Pour the batter into the lined tin and bake for 18–20 minutes. Leave to cool completely in the tin.

To serve, cut yourself a brownie – whatever size you feel is necessary – top with a scoop of ice cream, then quickly pour over your shot of hot espresso.

Makes about 12

**TIP** You should totally get creative with the ice cream you serve with dessert! You'll never hear me badmouthing vanilla, but it's fun to mix it up. This would be great with chocolate, salted caramel, caramelised almond, butter pecan – or even coffee ice cream for a double caffeine hit.

STREAMERS? CHECK. PARTY HATS? CHECK. GLITTER CANNON? OF COURSE! NOW ALL YOU NEED TO DO IS HIT THIS CHAPTER AND DECIDE WHICH RECIPE SUITS YOUR GRAND OCCASION. IT'S HARD TO DISAPPOINT WITH AN EPIC CANDY BAR LAYER CAKE (PAGE 130), BECAUSE IT IS EXACTLY WHAT IT SOUNDS LIKE. AND MY MIDSOMMAR BOMBE ALASKA (PAGE 118) WOULD DEFINITELY NOT BE OVERSHADOWED BY THAT TWO-STOREY JUMPING CASTLE YOU'RE PLANNING.

OK, SO MAYBE YOUR PARTY ISN'T QUITE SO MUCH OF AN EXTRAVAGANZA. BUT THIS IS STILL THE CHAPTER FOR YOU. GRADUATION, A NEW JOB, AN ENGAGEMENT, A WEDDING – THESE TO ME ARE ALL OPPORTUNITIES TO EAT AND TO MAKE SOMETHING DELICIOUS AND EXCITING. I'M ACTUALLY PRETTY TERRIBLE AT BIG PARTIES; MINGLING IS NOT MY FORTE. MY FAVOURITE KIND OF GATHERING IS WHATEVER A STEP DOWN FROM 'PARTY' IS – JUST A BUNCH OF FRIENDS OR FAMILY AROUND, EATING AND LAUGHING AND HANGING OUT.

I LIKE TO CELEBRATE IN A LOW-KEY WAY. MY DREAM WEDDING RECEPTION WOULD BE EVERYONE MUNCHING ON APPLE FRITTERS (PAGE 116) AND DRINKING HOT COFFEE ON A SNOW-COVERED MOUNTAIN SOMEWHERE IN THE ALPS. I LOVE TO END A DINNER WITH A GIANT, JIGGLING RHUBARB AND VANILLA BEAN JELLY (PAGE 124). AND I CAN'T IMAGINE A NICER WAY TO SAY CONGRATULATIONS THAN BY PRESENTING SOMEONE WITH THEIR OWN PERSONAL RASPBERRY, GINGER AND CHOCOLATE FLOAT (PAGE 133).

THESE ARE THE RECIPES THAT, TO ME, SAY 'THANK YOU', 'CONGRATULATIONS', 'WE'RE PROUD OF YOU' AND 'YOU MADE IT!'. AND THAT'S WHAT I WANT TO SAY WHEN I'M THROWING A PARTY. BECAUSE, NOT TO GET TOO DEEP WITH YOU HERE, BUT WE'RE HERE FOR A GOOD TIME, NOT A LONG TIME, AND I DON'T WANT TO MISS OUT ON A SINGLE CHANCE TO EAT COLA FLOAT ICE CREAM CAKE (PAGE 126) WITH THE PEOPLE I LOVE.

# BLACKBERRY RIPPLE CUSTARD DOUGHNUTS

*This recipe is a straight-up winner, and the secret, the magic ingredient is ... drumroll ... water! When these doughnuts hit the hot oil they puff up into the most ridiculously light, flavoursome doughnuts you can imagine.*

*DOUGHNUTS*
250 G (9 OZ/1⅔ CUPS) PLAIN (ALL-PURPOSE) FLOUR
2 TABLESPOONS CASTER (SUPERFINE) SUGAR, PLUS EXTRA FOR COATING
1 TEASPOON SALT
2 TEASPOONS DRY ACTIVE YEAST
2 EGGS
GRATED ZEST OF ½ LEMON
80 ML (2½ FL OZ/⅓ CUP) WARM WATER
65 G (2¼ OZ) BUTTER, SOFTENED
CANOLA OR GRAPESEED OIL FOR DEEP-FRYING

*FILLING*
2 EGG YOLKS
2 TABLESPOONS CASTER (SUPERFINE) SUGAR
1 TABLESPOON CORNFLOUR (CORNSTARCH)
125 ML (4 FL OZ/½ CUP) THICKENED (WHIPPING) CREAM (35% FAT)
125 ML (4 FL OZ/½ CUP) MILK
1 TEASPOON VANILLA BEAN PASTE
80 G (2¾ OZ/¼ CUP) SMOOTH BLACKBERRY JAM

For the doughnuts, put all the ingredients, except the butter and oil, in the bowl of a stand mixer fitted with the dough hook. Mix on low speed for about 4 minutes, or until combined and elastic. With the mixer running, add the butter, bit by bit, until incorporated. Scrape down the side of the bowl, cover with plastic wrap and set aside in a warm place to rise until doubled in size.

For the filling, in a small bowl, whisk together the egg yolks, caster sugar and cornflour.

Put the cream, milk and vanilla in a small saucepan over medium heat. When the milk begins to bubble around the edges, remove it from the heat and slowly whisk it into the egg mixture. Pour the mixture back into the pan and cook over medium heat, whisking constantly, until the mixture boils and becomes very thick – about 3 minutes. Once the mixture is the consistency of soft butter, scrape it into a bowl, cover and set aside to cool completely.

Punch the dough down and scrape it out onto a well-floured surface. Pat the dough into a rectangle, about 1 cm (½ in) thick, and cut out 9 doughnuts using a 7 cm (2¾ in) round cutter. Put the doughnuts on a baking tray lined with baking paper, cover with plastic wrap, and set aside to rise for another 45 minutes, or until puffy. Put 5 cm (2 in) of the oil in a saucepan over low heat (or use a deep-fryer) and heat the oil to 160°C (320°F) – when a small piece of dough dropped into the oil bubbles and rises to the surface, the oil is hot enough. Fry the doughnuts, a few at a time, for about 1 minute each side or until golden brown. Transfer to paper towel. Toss them in the extra caster sugar.

To fill the doughnuts, ripple the cold pastry cream with the jam. Press a piping (icing) bag fitted with a 5 mm (¼ in) nozzle into the side of each doughnut and squeeze until you can feel the weight of the doughnut increase slightly. Continue until all the doughnuts are filled. Serve.

*Makes 9*

WOULD YOU LOOK AT THE BEAUTY OF THIS CAKE? I CAN'T RESIST A RIPPLE, BUT THIS THING IS REALLY BEYOND. THE CAKE IS LATIN AMERICAN IN ORIGIN, ALSO KNOWN AS A TORTA DE TRES LECHES — THE 'TRES LECHES' REFERRING TO THE THREE DIFFERENT KINDS OF MILK THAT GO INTO THE CAKE (CONDENSED, EVAPORATED AND CREAM). THIS CAKE IS MOST REMINISCENT OF A TRIFLE, BUT IT'S SOMEHOW BOTH LIGHTER AND A LITTLE MORE LUSH. THE BLACKBERRY IS THE PERFECT SWEET-TART FOIL FOR THE SWEET, AIRY CAKE. IT'S BEST ENJOYED WHILE WEARING A FRIDA KAHLO-STYLE FLOWER CROWN.

*CAKE*
3 EGGS
170 G (6 OZ/¾ CUP) CASTER (SUPERFINE) SUGAR
1 TEASPOON VANILLA BEAN PASTE
110 G (4 OZ/¾ CUP) PLAIN (ALL-PURPOSE) FLOUR
1 TEASPOON BAKING POWDER
PINCH OF SALT

*SOAK*
60 ML (2 FL OZ/¼ CUP) CONDENSED MILK
60 ML (2 FL OZ/¼ CUP) POURING (SINGLE/LIGHT) CREAM (35% FAT)
60 ML (2 FL OZ/¼ CUP) EVAPORATED MILK

*TOPPING*
130 G (4½ OZ/1 CUP) BLACKBERRIES
2 TABLESPOONS CASTER (SUPERFINE) SUGAR
250 ML (8½ FL OZ/1 CUP) POURING (SINGLE/LIGHT) CREAM (35% FAT)

Preheat the oven to 180°C (350°F) and grease and line a 20 cm (8 in) square baking tin with baking paper.

To make the cake, put the eggs, sugar and vanilla in a bowl (or in the bowl of a stand mixer fitted with the whisk attachment) and whisk until mixture has tripled in volume and is almost white in colour. Turn off the mixer and sift in the flour, baking powder and salt. Fold together until the flour is completely incorporated.

Pour the batter into the tin and spread to the edges. Bake for 25–30 minutes, or until the cake springs back when touched lightly. Set aside to cool completely in the tin.

When the cake is cool, remove it from the tin and put it on a large, flat serving plate with a lip.

In a small pitcher, stir together the ingredients for the soak, then drizzle them slowly all over the cake. Cover the cake in plastic wrap and leave overnight in the refrigerator to soak.

Put the blackberries and sugar for the topping in a small saucepan over low heat, crush the blackberries slightly then cook until they are completely soft. Push them through a sieve to make a purée, then refrigerate overnight.

When you're ready to eat the cake, whip the cream to medium peaks and add half the blackberry purée, just barely rippling it through. Spread this over the top of the cake, drizzle over the remaining purée and serve.

Serves 8

*CALVADOS IS A COMPLETELY SEDUCTIVE APPLE BRANDY FROM FRANCE. I'VE READ THAT IT'S CONSIDERED A LITTLE BIT LAME OVER THERE, BUT I FIRST TASTED IT IN THE HOME OF FRENCH APPLES, NORMANDY, AND I LOVE IT NO MATTER WHAT. WHEN THAT APPLE-Y BOOZE IS COUPLED WITH CUSTARD-SOAKED, CRUNCHY-TOPPED, BUTTERY CROISSANTS AND CHUNKS OF APPLE, YOU HAVE A DESSERT PERFECT FOR ANY WINTER DINNER. JUST PLONK THIS ON THE TABLE AND LET PEOPLE SCOOP OUT THEIR OWN GREEDY PORTIONS. SERVE WITH ICE CREAM.*

```
6-8 CROISSANTS
2 APPLES (A TART VARIETY IS BEST), PEELED AND CUT INTO DICE
5 EGGS
115 G (4 OZ/½ CUP) CASTER (SUPERFINE) SUGAR
60 ML (2 FL OZ/¼ CUP) CALVADOS
310 ML (10½ FL OZ/1¼ CUPS) MILK
250 ML (8½ FL OZ/1 CUP) THICKENED (WHIPPING) CREAM (35% FAT)
25 G (1 OZ/¼ CUP) FLAKED ALMONDS
ICING (CONFECTIONERS') SUGAR FOR DUSTING (OPTIONAL)
```

Tear the croissants into chunks and spread them in a shallow baking dish with the apple chunks.

In a bowl, whisk together the eggs, caster sugar and calvados, then stir in the milk and cream.

Pour the custard mixture over the croissants, cover the dish with plastic wrap and leave to soak for at least 15 minutes (or a couple of hours) in the refrigerator.

Preheat the oven to 180°C (350°F).

Scatter the flaked almonds over the pudding and bake for about 25 minutes or until golden and set, with a bit of a wobble in the centre. Dust with icing sugar, if desired.

Serves 6–8

*THIS RECIPE IS INSPIRED BY THAT UBIQUITOUS VERSION OF THE BAVARIAN THAT EXISTS IN SUPERMARKET FREEZERS AROUND THE WORLD. IT MAKES ME THINK OF BEING A TEENAGER, JUST COMING INTO THE FREEDOM OF HAVING A CAR (OR MY SISTER HAVING A CAR) AND HAVING SOME MONEY OF MY OWN. WEIRDLY, THE THING MY SISTER AND I WOULD SPEND OUR MONEY ON WAS FROZEN CHOCOLATE BAVARIAN, BUT I DON'T JUDGE US. MY RECIPE IS LIKE THAT OLD-SCHOOL BAVARIAN, JUST AMPED UP WITH A GOOD-QUALITY CHOCOLATE AND NO WEIRD CHEMICALS. I HOPE YOU EAT IT OUT OF THE PAN WITH YOUR SISTER AND TWO FORKS.*

*BASE*
250 G (9 OZ) BUTTERNUT SNAP COOKIES (OR DIGESTIVES OR GRAHAM CRACKERS)
50 G (1¾ OZ) BUTTER, SOFTENED
PINCH OF SALT

*FILLING*
375 ML (12½ FL OZ/1½ CUPS) FULL-CREAM (WHOLE) MILK
1 TABLESPOON POWDERED GELATINE
115 G (4 OZ/½ CUP) CASTER (SUPERFINE) SUGAR
30 G (1 OZ/¼ CUP) UNSWEETENED (DUTCH) COCOA POWDER
50 G (1¾ OZ) MILK CHOCOLATE (60% COCOA SOLIDS)
250 ML (8½ FL OZ/1 CUP) POURING (SINGLE/LIGHT) CREAM (35% FAT)

*TO SERVE*
250 ML (8½ FL OZ/1 CUP) POURING (SINGLE/LIGHT) CREAM (35% FAT)
CHOCOLATE FLAKES (OPTIONAL)
MARASCHINO CHERRIES (OPTIONAL)

Grease and line a 20 cm (8 in) round springform cake tin with baking paper.

To make the base, put the cookies and butter in a food processor and blitz until finely ground and the mixture looks like damp sand. Dump the mixture into the tin and press down so that you have a compact base layer. Put in the refrigerator to set while you make the filling.

For the filling, put 125 ml (4 fl oz/½ cup) of the milk in a small bowl and sprinkle over the gelatine. Stir together and set aside.

Put the remaining milk, the sugar and cocoa in a medium saucepan over medium–high heat and bring to the boil, whisking continuously. Once the mixture boils, turn off the heat, let any bubbles subside and then whisk in the gelatine mixture – it should dissolve immediately. Add the chocolate and stir until melted. Pour the mixture into a bowl and put it in the refrigerator to chill for 30 minutes.

Once the mixture is chilled, whip the cream to stiff peaks, and then fold through the chilled mixture – the filling will be pretty much liquid, so this will seem impossible, but just keep folding until everything is incorporated. Pour the filling into the cookie-lined tin, and refrigerate for 4 hours or overnight.

To serve, carefully run a knife around the edge of the tin and unmould the bavarian. Whip the cream to soft peaks and slather over the top of the bavarian. Decorate with chocolate flakes and maraschino cherries, if desired.

Serves 6–8

# APPLE FRITTERS

*NOTHING SAYS PARTY LIKE A FRITTER - ESPECIALLY THIS MEGA-BATCH OF STURDY, PUFFY, APPLE-FILLED WONDERS. THESE ARE PERFECT TO MAKE FOR ANY TIME YOU HAVE A BUNCH OF PEOPLE AT YOUR PLACE, JUST HANGING OUT. WHETHER YOU'RE WATCHING THE CRICKET, THE SUPER BOWL, THE OSCARS OR THE NORTHERN LIGHTS, I CAN THINK OF NO NICER THING TO EAT THAN A MUNCHY, SUGAR-CRUSTED FRITTER. BUT YOU SHOULD DEFINITELY WAIT UNTIL YOU HAVE A CROWD OVER. I SAY THIS BECAUSE I FEEL THAT, UNLESS YOU HAVE A BUNCH OF CLOSE FRIENDS WHO WILL HOOVER THESE UP (WITH ABSOLUTE JOY - THEY'RE AMAZING), THEN YOU SHOULD NOT MAKE THEM. IT WOULD BE FAR TOO DANGEROUS TO HAVE A BATCH ALL TO YOURSELF.*

450 G (1 LB/3 CUPS) PLAIN (ALL-PURPOSE) FLOUR
55 G (2 OZ/¼ CUP) CASTER (SUPERFINE) SUGAR, PLUS EXTRA FOR COATING
1 TABLESPOON DRY ACTIVE YEAST
PINCH OF SALT
1 TEASPOON GROUND CINNAMON
½ TEASPOON FRESHLY GRATED NUTMEG
1 TEASPOON VANILLA BEAN PASTE
250 ML (8½ FL OZ/1 CUP) MILK
2 EGGS
2 APPLES
GRAPESEED OR CANOLA OIL FOR DEEP-FRYING

Put all the ingredients, except the apples and oil, in the bowl of a stand mixer fitted with the dough hook. Beat on low speed until the mixture comes together as a thick, sticky dough.

Peel and chop the apples into small, 1 cm (½ in) dice, then add them to the dough, stirring to incorporate – don't worry if it seems like the dough isn't holding them. Cover the bowl with plastic wrap and set aside to rise for an hour, or until doubled in size.

When the dough has risen, fill a deep saucepan over medium heat with about 5 cm (2 in) oil. Heat the oil to 160°C (320°F) – if a small piece of fritter dough rises to the surface and starts bubbling gently in the oil when you drop it in, the oil is hot enough. Take any old spoon and scoop generous portions of the dough into the oil, about 3 or 4 at a time. Fry for 1–2 minutes on each side, or until golden brown and cooked through. Transfer to a wire rack over some paper towel, to drain.

When all the fritters are cooked, toss them a few at a time in a bowl of caster sugar to coat.

**Makes about 20**

*I HAVE A MORE THAN MILD OBSESSION WITH THE SCANDINAVIAN COUNTRIES. I'VE NEVER BEEN, BUT I'M DESPERATE TO GO. I LOVE THEIR DESIGN, THE LANDSCAPE, THE COFFEE-CULTURE AND, ESPECIALLY, THE FOOD. MIDSOMMAR IS SWEDISH FOR, YOU GUESSED IT, MIDSUMMER, AND IT'S ALSO A HUGE CELEBRATION, WHICH FEATURES PICKLED HERRING, FLOWER CROWNS, PLENTY OF AQUAVIT AND A HUGE BERRY-COVERED MIDSOMMAR CAKE. THIS IS MY FANCY TAKE ON THAT CAKE, WHICH BRINGS THE SNOW-COVERED WINTER AND THE SUNNY SUMMER OF SWEDEN TOGETHER IN ONE DESSERT.*

1/2 BATCH CUPCAKE BATTER FROM STRAWBERRY AND ROSE BUTTERFLY CAKES
 (PAGE 40)
750 ML (25 1/2 FL OZ/3 CUPS) VANILLA ICE CREAM
500 ML (17 FL OZ/2 CUPS) RASPBERRY SORBET

*MERINGUE*
3 EGG WHITES
230 G (8 OZ/1 CUP) CASTER (SUPERFINE) SUGAR

Preheat the oven to 180°C (350°F) and grease and line an 18 cm (7 in) round springform cake tin with baking paper.

Scrape the batter into the tin and bake for 15–20 minutes, or until the cake springs back when touched lightly. Let the cake cool in the tin for 10 minutes, then transfer to a wire rack to cool completely.

Line a 1.5 litre (51 fl oz/6 cup) pudding basin (or any bowl/mould – the taller the better, as long as it will fit in your freezer) with several layers of plastic wrap.

Soften the ice cream and sorbet at room temperature for just a few minutes, then scoop and layer them into the lined basin. Cover with plastic wrap and put in the freezer for at least 4 hours to set solid.

When you're ready to serve, make the meringue. Put the egg whites in the bowl of a stand mixer, fitted with the whisk attachment.

Put the sugar and 60 ml (2 fl oz/¼ cup) water in a small saucepan over medium heat and bring to the boil, without stirring. Using a sugar thermometer, cook the mixture until it reaches 115°C (240°F), then turn off the heat and set the pan aside.

Immediately begin whisking the egg whites on high speed until they reach soft peaks. Turn the mixer down to medium–low and carefully stream in the hot sugar syrup. Once all the syrup is in, turn the mixer back up to high and whisk until the meringue is cool, about 15–20 minutes.

Put the cake on a cake stand. Unmould the frozen ice cream mound on top of it, removing any plastic. If necessary, trim the edge of the cake so that it's flush with the ice cream. Mound the cooled meringue all over the ice cream and cake, and spread with a spatula or palette knife, making plenty of swirls as you go. You can serve it as is, or carefully use a kitchen blowtorch to brown the outside of the meringue. Cut into slices with a hot knife and serve.

Serves 8

# CHERRY BROWNIE STRUDEL

*I WAS INSPIRED TO MAKE THIS RIDICULOUSLY SIMPLE, BUT TOTALLY SHOW-STOPPING, STRUDEL AFTER SEEING A RECIPE BY THE MAN HIMSELF, JAMIE OLIVER, FOR A LEFT-OVER CHRISTMAS PUDDING VERSION. I LOVED THE IDEA OF A MOLTEN, DELICIOUS FILLING, ENCASED IN LIGHT, CRISP FILO PASTRY. BUT, BECAUSE I HAVE NO RESTRAINT AND DON'T KNOW WHEN TO STOP, I NIXED THE CHRISTMAS PUDDING AND REPLACED IT WITH CRUMBLED CHOCOLATE BROWNIES AND TART, JUICY CHERRIES. THE BROWNIES FOR THIS NEED TO COME FROM A PREDOMINANTLY CHOCOLATE RECIPE, TO GET THE REQUISITE LEVEL OF GOO AND CHEW. THE RECIPE ON PAGE 104 IS ABSOLUTELY PERFECT FOR THIS – YOU'LL NEED ABOUT THREE-QUARTERS OF A BATCH. SERVE WITH CRÈME FRAÎCHE OR DOUBLE (THICK/HEAVY) CREAM.*

6 SHEETS OF FILO PASTRY
50 G (1¾ OZ) BUTTER, MELTED
RAW (DEMERARA) SUGAR FOR SPRINKLING
450 G (1 LB) VERY CHOCOLATEY BROWNIES (SEE PAGE 104)
200 G (7 OZ/1 CUP) PITTED MORELLO CHERRIES, DRAINED

Preheat the oven to 200°C (400°F) and line a baking tray with baking paper.

Lay 2 sheets of filo pastry on a clean work surface and overlap them so that they form a large square. Brush liberally with melted butter, being sure to brush the overlapping seam so they stick together. Sprinkle over some sugar and top with 2 more sheets of pastry – but give them a 90-degree turn, so that the seam of these 2 sheets forms a cross with the first layer. Brush again with butter, sprinkle over a little more sugar, and top with the final 2 sheets of filo pastry, placing them in the same direction as the first layer. Brush with butter.

Crumble over the brownies, then scatter over the cherries, leaving a 5 cm (2 in) border around the edge of the pastry. Fold the 2 sides in and then roll up the strudel into a log, encasing the brownies and cherries.

Carefully transfer the strudel to the baking tray. Brush with any remaining butter and give it a final sprinkling of sugar. Bake for 25–30 minutes or until golden brown.

Serves 6

*CHOCOLATE AND LIME IS A SLEEPER COMBINATION, BUT IT'S A WINNER. THINK CHEESECAKE, MEETS KEY LIME PIE WITH A CHOCOLATE CRUST.*

75 G (2¾ OZ) BUTTER
250 ML (8½ FL OZ/1 CUP) BREWED COFFEE
2 TEASPOONS VANILLA BEAN PASTE
345 G (12 OZ/1½ CUPS) CASTER (SUPERFINE) SUGAR
185 G (6½ OZ/1¼ CUPS) PLAIN (ALL-PURPOSE) FLOUR
90 G (3 OZ/¾ CUP) UNSWEETENED (DUTCH) COCOA POWDER
2½ TEASPOONS BAKING POWDER
1½ TEASPOONS BICARBONATE OF SODA (BAKING SODA)
PINCH OF SALT
250 G (9 OZ/1 CUP) SOUR CREAM
3 LARGE EGGS
150 G (5½ OZ) DARK CHOCOLATE (70% COCOA SOLIDS)
125 ML (4 FL OZ/½ CUP) POURING (SINGLE/LIGHT) CREAM (35% FAT)
1 TABLESPOON LIQUID GLUCOSE (OR CORN SYRUP)
CRUMBLED CHOCOLATE COOKIES

*CHEESECAKE FILLING*
125 ML (4 FL OZ/½ CUP) THICKENED (WHIPPING) CREAM (35% FAT)
500 G (1 LB 2 OZ/2 CUPS) CREAM CHEESE, SOFTENED
170 G (6 OZ/¾ CUP) CASTER (SUPERFINE) SUGAR
190 ML (6½ FL OZ/¾ CUP) LIME JUICE (FROM ABOUT 6 LIMES)
GRATED ZEST OF 2 LIMES
80 ML (2½ FL OZ/⅓ CUP) CONDENSED MILK
1 TABLESPOON POWDERED GELATINE
45 ML (1½ FL OZ) BOILING WATER

Preheat the oven to 180°C (350°F) and grease and line three 20 cm (8 in) springform cake tins. Put the butter, coffee and vanilla in a saucepan over medium heat and cook until the butter is melted. Put the sugar, flour, cocoa, baking powder, bicarbonate of soda and salt in a mixing bowl and whisk (sift the cocoa if it's lumpy). Add the coffee mixture, sour cream and eggs and whisk until combined. Divide the mixture between the tins and bake for 20–25 minutes or until the cakes spring back when touched lightly. Leave to cool for 10 minutes in the tins, then transfer to wire racks to cool completely. Use a serrated knife to level off the cakes.

For the filling, whip the cream to soft peaks. Beat together the cream cheese and sugar until smooth and combined. Beat in the lime juice, zest and condensed milk. Put the gelatine in a small bowl, add the boiling water and mix to dissolve the gelatine. While beating the cream cheese mixture, stream in the gelatine until incorporated (do this quickly). Fold through the whipped cream.

Line an 18 cm (7 in) springform tin with acetate (see page 9). Trim the cake layers down to 18 cm (7 in) and put one layer in the tin, followed by half the cheesecake filling. Follow with another cake layer, the remaining filling and then the final piece of cake. Refrigerate for at least 6 hours or overnight. To decorate, unclip the tin, peel away the acetate and place the cake on a serving plate. Melt together the chocolate, cream and glucose in a saucepan over low heat. Cool slightly. Pour over the cake, then scatter a ring of cookie crumbs around the top edge.

Serves 8

# RHUBARB AND VANILLA BEAN JELLY

*THIS JELLY WILL CHANGE EVERY IDEA YOU'VE EVER HAD ABOUT JELLY FOR DESSERT, ESPECIALLY IF YOU'VE ONLY EVER HAD THE STUFF MADE FROM CRYSTALS. THIS JELLY IS PURE, SWEET RHUBARB FLAVOUR PERFUMED WITH VANILLA. IT IS FULLY, RIDICULOUSLY, ELECTRICALLY PINK. IT'S JUST SO INTENSE IN EVERY WAY, I ABSOLUTELY LOVE IT. THIS IS THE STEVIE NICKS OF DESSERTS. SERVE WITH CRÈME FRAÎCHE OR WHIPPED CREAM.*

900 G (2 LB) RHUBARB (TRIMMED WEIGHT)
345 G (12 OZ/1½ CUPS) CASTER (SUPERFINE) SUGAR
1 VANILLA BEAN, SPLIT LENGTHWAYS AND SEEDS SCRAPED
18 G (¾ OZ) TITANIUM-STRENGTH GELATINE LEAVES

Chop the rhubarb into 2 cm (¾ in) pieces and put it in a large saucepan over medium–low heat with the sugar, vanilla bean and seeds and 750 ml (25½ fl oz/3 cups) water. Put the lid on, bring to the boil and cook for about 5 minutes, or until the rhubarb is very soft.

Once cooked, strain the mixture through a sieve into a large measuring pitcher. You should get about 1 litre (34 fl oz/4 cups) of liquid – if there's not quite enough you can top it up with water or a squeeze of orange juice – or even pomegranate juice, if you have some.

Put the gelatine leaves in a shallow bowl, cover with cold water and soak for 5 minutes.

Put 250 ml (8½ fl oz/1 cup) of the rhubarb liquid in a small saucepan over low heat. Once the rhubarb juice is steaming hot, turn off the heat, squeeze out the gelatine leaves (now turned to goo), and whisk them into the hot liquid until they're dissolved.

Stir the dissolved gelatine–rhubarb mixture back into the main rhubarb pitcher, then pour into a lightly greased 1 litre (34 fl oz/4 cup) jelly mould. Refrigerate for at least 6 hours or overnight.

**Serves 6**

**TIP** The left-over rhubarb is still delicious – use it to make a rhubarb fool (sweeten the left-over rhubarb to taste then fold through whipped cream), or to eat for breakfast with some Supa-thick yoghurt (page 18).

# COLA FLOAT ICE CREAM CAKE

MY LOVE OF ICE CREAM FLOATS (OR 'SPIDERS' AS THEY ARE KNOWN IN MY FAMILY) IS WELL DOCUMENTED. ACTUALLY, I'VE INCLUDED ONE IN THIS CHAPTER (PAGE 133). BUT I COULDN'T RESIST THE DESIRE TO LEVEL-UP THE FLOAT TO A FULLY-FLEDGED ICE CREAM CAKE. AND HOW COULD I WRITE A BOOK CALLED THE SUGAR HIT WITHOUT INCLUDING POP ROCKS AT SOME POINT? THAT'S RIGHT, POP ROCKS! THIS CAKE IS A PARTY-STARTER, FOR SURE.

200 G (7 OZ/1⅓ CUPS) PLAIN (ALL-PURPOSE) FLOUR
40 G (1½ OZ/⅓ CUP) UNSWEETENED (DUTCH) COCOA POWDER
285 G (10 OZ/1¼ CUPS) CASTER (SUPERFINE) SUGAR
½ TEASPOON BAKING POWDER
PINCH OF SALT
1 TEASPOON MIXED SPICE
115 G (4 OZ) BUTTER
170 ML (5½ FL OZ/⅔ CUP) COLA
1 EGG
125 ML (4 FL OZ/½ CUP) BUTTERMILK
1 TEASPOON VANILLA BEAN PASTE

FILLING AND DECORATION
1 LITRE (34 FL OZ/4 CUPS) VANILLA ICE CREAM
125 ML (4 FL OZ/½ CUP) POURING (SINGLE/LIGHT) CREAM (35% FAT)
2 TABLESPOONS LIQUID GLUCOSE (OR CORN SYRUP)
150 G (5½ OZ) DARK CHOCOLATE (70% COCOA SOLIDS)
2 PACKETS COLA POP ROCKS (OR STRAWBERRY IS GOOD TOO)

Preheat the oven to 180°C (350°F) and grease and line an 18 cm (7 in) cake tin.

Put the flour, cocoa, sugar, baking powder, salt and mixed spice in a large mixing bowl.

Put the butter and cola in a saucepan over medium heat and cook until the butter is melted.

Add the hot mixture to the dry ingredients in the bowl and stir through. Finally, add the egg, buttermilk and vanilla and stir until smooth and combined. Pour the mixture into the tin and bake for 40 minutes, or until risen and a skewer inserted into the centre comes out clean. Remove the cake carefully from the tin after about 10 minutes and transfer to a wire rack to cool completely.

When you're ready to assemble, take the ice cream out of the refrigerator to soften.

Line an 18 cm (7 in) cake tin with two or three layers of plastic wrap.

Trim the cake and slice it horizontally into two even layers. Put the bottom layer in the tin, then spread over the ice cream. Top with the final piece of cake, cover with plastic wrap and put back in the freezer to set for at least 4 hours.

When you're ready to serve, melt together the cream, glucose and chocolate in a small saucepan over low heat, stirring constantly. Unmould the cake and place it on a serving plate. Drizzle over the sauce, leave for a minute to set, then sprinkle over the pop rocks. Serve in wedges with any left-over sauce on the side.

Serves 8

*IN MY HEAD, I CALL THIS 'STREET FIGHTER PIE', BECAUSE IT'S BLACK AND BLUE (GEDDIT?), AND BECAUSE IT SOUNDS SO BADASS. ASIDE FROM THAT, THIS PIE HAS AN AWFUL LOT GOING FOR IT. IT SERVES A CROWD EASILY AND IT'S DELICIOUS IN THE WAY THAT ONLY A FLAKY-CRUSTED BERRY PIE CAN BE. IN A CARTOON WORLD THE SMELL ALONE WOULD BE ENOUGH TO MAKE YOU FLOAT TO WHATEVER WINDOW SILL THIS WAS COOLING ON. IT'S ALSO A CRUST-HEAVY PIE, AND I HAPPEN TO BE A LOVER OF CRUST. THINK 'GIANT POP TART' AND YOU'VE PRETTY MUCH GOT THE GIST.*

*DOUGH*
900 G (2 LB/6 CUPS) PLAIN (ALL-PURPOSE) FLOUR
2 TABLESPOONS CASTER (SUPERFINE) SUGAR
1 TEASPOON SALT
450 G (1 LB) BUTTER, COLD
170 ML (5½ FL OZ/⅔ CUP) ICED WATER
1 EGG, BEATEN

*FILLING*
360 G (12½ OZ) FRESH OR FROZEN BLACKBERRIES
620 G (1 LB 6 OZ/4 CUPS) FRESH OR FROZEN BLUEBERRIES
170 G (6 OZ/¾ CUP) CASTER (SUPERFINE) SUGAR
30 G (1 OZ/¼ CUP) CORNFLOUR (CORNSTARCH)
GRATED ZEST AND JUICE OF 1 LEMON
1 TEASPOON GROUND CINNAMON

To make the dough, put the flour, sugar and salt in the bowl of a stand mixer fitted with the paddle attachment. Cut the butter into cubes and add it to the mixer. Mix on low speed until the mixture starts to look like breadcrumbs, with some larger flakes and pieces of butter still visible. With the mixer on medium speed, stream in enough of the iced water to make the dough look like it's about to come together (you may not need all of it). Squidge the dough into 2 pieces and flatten these out roughly into thick rectangles. Wrap in plastic wrap and put in the refrigerator for at least 30 minutes.

When you're ready to bake, preheat the oven to 200°C (400°F) and lightly grease a 26 x 40 cm (10¼ x 16 in) baking dish. Remove one of the pieces of dough from the refrigerator and roll it out on a well-floured work surface – you want a rectangle about 5 mm (¼ in) thick, and about 5 cm (2 in) larger than the baking dish. Flour the top of the dough, then fold it into quarters. Transfer it to the baking dish and carefully unfold it. If the dough tears, just squish it back together. Trim the edges of the dough and save the offcuts.

Toss together all the filling ingredients in a large bowl, then spread the mixture over the dough in the baking dish.

Repeat the rolling process with the second piece of dough, and use it to top the pie – again trimming the dough and saving the offcuts. Crimp the edges of the pie together, then brush it with beaten egg.

Use the offcuts to make any decorations you like (I like a scattering of stars), then stick them on the pie and brush them with a little more egg. Put the pie in the oven and reduce the heat to 180°C (350°F). Bake for 50–60 minutes, or until the pie is deep golden and bubbling.

Serves 16–20

**TIP** This recipe makes A LOT of crust. I wrote the recipe that way to give you plenty of leeway when rolling out such big sheets of dough – it can be tricky. If you're confident, you could easily make do with three-quarters of this amount. But extra dough does mean there's plenty left over for decorations.

*FOR THE TIMES WHEN NOTHING BUT AN EPIC CAKE WILL DO, I GIVE YOU THE EPIC CANDY BAR LAYER CAKE! LAYERS OF CHOCOLATE SOUR CREAM CAKE, MALTED CHOCOLATE FROSTING, SALTED CARAMEL AND CHOPPED-UP MINI CANDY BARS. THIS IS THE BIRTHDAY CAKE OF MY DREAMS.*

75 G (2¾ OZ) BUTTER
250 ML (8½ FL OZ/1 CUP) BREWED COFFEE
2 TEASPOONS VANILLA BEAN PASTE
345 G (12 OZ/1½ CUPS) CASTER (SUPERFINE) SUGAR
185 G (6½ OZ/1¼ CUPS) PLAIN (ALL-PURPOSE) FLOUR
90 G (3 OZ/¾ CUP) UNSWEETENED (DUTCH) COCOA POWDER
2½ TEASPOONS BAKING POWDER
1½ TEASPOONS BICARBONATE OF SODA (BAKING SODA)
PINCH OF SALT
250 G (9 OZ/1 CUP) SOUR CREAM
3 EGGS

*MALT FROSTING*
225 G (8 OZ) BUTTER, SOFTENED
150 G (5½ OZ/1½ CUPS) MALTED DRINK POWDER (OVALTINE OR HORLICKS)
375 G (13 OZ/3 CUPS) ICING (CONFECTIONERS') SUGAR
150 G (5½ OZ) DARK CHOCOLATE (70% COCOA SOLIDS), MELTED AND
  COOLED SLIGHTLY
45 G (1½ OZ) SOUR CREAM

*TO DECORATE*
½ BATCH SALTED CARAMEL (PAGE 9), COMPLETELY COOLED
CHOPPED MINI CANDY BARS, TO DECORATE (SNICKERS, TWIX, MARS, MALTESERS,
  M&MS OR PEANUT BUTTER CUPS ARE GOOD CHOICES)

Preheat the oven to 180°C (350°F) and grease and line three 18 cm (7 in) round springform cake tins. Put the butter, coffee and vanilla in a saucepan over medium heat and cook until the butter is melted. Put the sugar, flour, cocoa, baking powder, bicarbonate of soda and salt in a large mixing bowl and whisk together (you might want to sift the cocoa if it's super lumpy). Add the coffee–butter mixture, sour cream and eggs and whisk until everything is combined. Divide the mixture between the three tins and bake for 20–25 minutes or until the cakes spring back when touched lightly. Leave to cool for at least 10 minutes in the tins, then transfer to wire racks to cool completely. Use a serrated knife to level off the cakes, if they're domed.

To make the malt frosting, put the butter in the bowl of a stand mixer and beat with the paddle attachment until light and creamy. Add the malted drink powder and icing sugar and beat again until incorporated – it may look a little dry, but that's OK. While mixing on low speed, stream in the melted chocolate and beat until incorporated. Finally, beat in the sour cream. To assemble, place a layer of cake on a stand and dollop on a third of the frosting. Spread it messily across. Drizzle with a little salted caramel and scatter over some chopped candy bars. Repeat with the next 2 layers, finishing with a final scattering of candy pieces. If you need to, anchor the cake with a few skewers. Refrigerate until ready to serve.

*Serves 8*

WHAT IS A PARTY WITHOUT A DRINK? EVERY TIME I HAVE A FRIEND, LOVED ONE OR EVEN JUST A BUNCH OF STRANGERS AROUND ME, I WANT A GLASS OF SOMETHING DELICIOUS IN MY HAND. IT COULD BE SOMETHING BOOZY, LIKE MY QUEENSLANDER TAKE ON THE DARK AND STORMY, FEATURING ALL THREE OF OUR BIGGEST TRADEMARKS – PINEAPPLES, RUM AND GINGER BEER – OR A SUPER-SWANKY PASSIONFRUIT CHAMPAGNE FLOAT. OR FOR THE TIMES WHEN IT'S JUST A PARTY IN A GLASS THAT YOU'RE AFTER, WHY NOT A RASPBERRY, GINGER AND CHOCOLATE FLOAT OR A CUP OF THICK PEANUT BUTTER HOT CHOCOLATE? LET'S STEP OUR PARTY-DRINK GAME UP A NOTCH.

## QUEENSLAND DARK AND STORMY

750 ML (25½ FL OZ/3 CUPS) GINGER BEER
375 ML (12½ FL OZ/1½ CUPS) PINEAPPLE JUICE
125 ML (4 FL OZ/½ CUP) LIME JUICE, OR TO TASTE
4–6 SHOTS OF DARK RUM
ICE CUBES
SLICED LIMES, TO SERVE

Combine all the ingredients in a large pitcher or punchbowl with plenty of ice. Serve with slices of lime.

Serves 4

## PASSIONFRUIT CHAMPAGNE FLOAT (AKA #PASHTAG)

500 ML (17 FL OZ/2 CUPS) STORE-BOUGHT PASSIONFRUIT SORBET
1 X 750 ML (25½ FL OZ) BOTTLE CHAMPAGNE (OR PROSECCO OR SPARKLING WINE)

I think you know where I'm going with this. Put a scoop of sorbet in each glass and top it up with your fizz of choice.

Serves 6–8

# RASPBERRY, GINGER AND CHOCOLATE FLOAT

200 G (7 OZ/1²/₃ CUPS) RASPBERRIES
1 TABLESPOON CASTER (SUPERFINE) SUGAR
1 TEASPOON VANILLA BEAN PASTE
4 SCOOPS OF VANILLA ICE CREAM
4 SCOOPS OF CHOCOLATE ICE CREAM
2 X 375 ML (12¹/₂ FL OZ) BOTTLES GOOD, SPICY GINGER BEER

Put the raspberries, sugar and vanilla in a small saucepan over medium heat and bring to the boil. As soon as the mixture boils, turn off the heat and set aside to cool. (This mix can be made ahead of time and kept in the refrigerator for up to 3 days. It also freezes perfectly.)

To assemble the floats, divide the raspberry sauce between four tall glasses. Put a scoop each of vanilla and chocolate ice cream in the glasses, then bring them to the table. Top up each glass with half a bottle of ginger beer, watch the glasses fizz over and dig in!

Serves 4

# THICK PEANUT BUTTER HOT CHOCOLATE

500 ML (17 FL OZ/2 CUPS) MILK
2 TEASPOONS CORNFLOUR (CORNSTARCH)
2 TEASPOONS UNSWEETENED (DUTCH) COCOA POWDER
50 G (1³/₄ OZ) MILK CHOCOLATE (50-60% COCOA SOLIDS)
25 G (1 OZ) DARK CHOCOLATE (70% COCOA SOLIDS)
60 G (2 OZ/¹/₄ CUP) SMOOTH PEANUT BUTTER
WHIPPED CREAM, TO SERVE (OPTIONAL)
PRETZELS, TO SERVE (OPTIONAL)

Take a tablespoon of the milk and mix it together with the cornstarch in a small bowl. Set aside.

Put the remaining milk and the rest of the ingredients in a medium saucepan over low heat. Heat the mixture slowly, whisking gently but constantly, until the chocolate and peanut butter are melted and the mixture is steaming – don't let it boil. Whisk in the cornflour mixture and continue to heat until the mixture thickens slightly.

Pour the hot chocolate into two mugs and top with whipped cream and a crunchy pretzel, if desired.

Serves 2

CANDY CANES, CHRISTMAS CRACKERS, TREES, BAUBLES, PUDDINGS, TURKEYS, HAM, CROWNS AND CAROLS! I AM ALWAYS SO OVER-THE-TOP EXCITED ABOUT THE HOLIDAY SEASON. I'M FREAKING BUDDY THE ELF! WHEN THE DECORATIONS START APPEARING IN THE SHOPS, I'M SO HAPPY TO SEE THEM. I HAVE NO TIME FOR HOLIDAY HATERZ. WHAT'S TO HATE? IT'S A SEASON OF ALL THE BEST FOOD, FRIENDS, INDULGENCE AND FUN, AND YOU GET TO PUT UP A GIANT, SPANGLY TREE IN YOUR HOUSE. THAT, TO ME, IS A RECIPE FOR A GOOD TIME.

I CHOOSE TO EMBRACE THE CHRISTMAS TRADITION, BECAUSE THAT'S WHAT I WAS BROUGHT UP WITH, BUT THAT DOESN'T MEAN YOU WON'T FIND SOMETHING PERFECT FOR HANUKKAH, KWANZAA OR, HEY, EVEN FESTIVUS IN THIS CHAPTER.

I TOTALLY HAVE MY PARENTS TO BLAME FOR MY CHRISTMAS GLEE. THEY KICK ASS AT CHRISTMAS, AND MADE IT INCREDIBLY AWESOME FOR ME AND MY BROTHER AND SISTER WHEN WE WERE GROWING UP. WE ALWAYS HAD A GIGANTIC TREE, WITH A TRAIN CHUGGING AROUND THE BASE, AND LITTLE CHRISTMAS TOWNS SET UP ON EVERY AVAILABLE SURFACE THROUGHOUT THE HOUSE. WEEKS OF READING CHRISTMAS BOOKS BEFORE BED – CLASSICS LIKE HOW THE GRINCH STOLE CHRISTMAS, THE POLAR EXPRESS, THE NUTCRACKER AND A BEAUTIFUL COPY OF THE NIGHT BEFORE CHRISTMAS – WOULD GET US SO EXCITED FOR THE BIG DAY, YOU COULD FEEL THE MAGIC IN THE AIR. ON CHRISTMAS EVE WE WOULD HEAR SLEIGH BELLS JINGLING OUTSIDE OUR BEDROOM, AND I AM LUCKY ENOUGH TO HAVE HAD MIDNIGHT SANTA-SIGHTINGS ON AT LEAST TWO OCCASIONS. WE ALWAYS LEFT OUT COOKIES (AND OCCASIONALLY A BEER) FOR SANTA, AND CARROTS FOR THE REINDEER. TO THIS DAY MY PARENTS MAINTAIN THAT HE SENDS US PRESENTS EVERY YEAR, AND I HAVE NO REASON TO SUSPECT IT'S NOT TRUE.

THE HOLIDAYS, TO ME, ARE ALL ABOUT EMBRACING THE SPIRIT OF THE SEASON. LIKE ANYTHING, YOU CAN CHOOSE TO FOCUS ON THE CRUDDY PARTS, THE COMMERCIALISATION AND FORCED SOCIAL INTERACTION, BUT I PREFER TO SQUISH THAT TOO-SMALL PAPER CROWN ONTO MY HEAD AND ENJOY THE OCCASION. EVEN NOW, CHRISTMAS EVE IS MY FAVOURITE DAY OF THE YEAR – IT'S WHEN THAT CRACKLE OF MAGIC IS THE STRONGEST IN THE AIR. NOW LET'S CRAM SOME ICE CREAM BETWEEN TWO MINCE PIES, MAKE OUR BREAD PUDDING TASTE LIKE EGGNOG AND DO THIS THING RIGHT!

# FESTIVE GRANOLA

*This is my favourite granola of all time. I mean, I love my Blueberry pancake granola (page 26), but I also do try to exercise a little restraint when I'm making it, going easy on the sugar and fat. This festive granola, on the other hand, tastes like cookies and sleigh bells and mistletoe and pure unadulterated Christmas joy.*

300 G (10½ OZ/3 CUPS) WHOLE ROLLED (PORRIDGE) OATS
100 G (3½ OZ/1 CUP) PECANS
90 (3 OZ/1 CUP) FLAKED ALMONDS (SKIN ON, IF YOU CAN)
60 G (2 OZ/½ CUP) CHIA SEEDS
50 G (1¾ OZ) BUTTER, MELTED
55 G (1 OZ/¼ CUP, FIRMLY PACKED) BROWN SUGAR
125 ML (4 FL OZ/½ CUP) MAPLE SYRUP
1 TEASPOON VANILLA BEAN PASTE
2 TEASPOONS GROUND CINNAMON
½ TEASPOON GROUND GINGER
PINCH OF SALT
145 G (5 OZ/1 CUP) DRIED CRANBERRIES (CRAISINS)

Preheat the oven to 180°C (350°F) and line two baking trays with baking paper.

Put the oats, pecans, almonds and chia seeds in a large bowl and stir to combine.

In a measuring pitcher, whisk together the melted butter, brown sugar, maple syrup, vanilla, cinnamon, ginger and salt.

Pour the liquid mixture into the dry ingredients and stir together very well.

Dump the mixture onto the lined baking trays and spread out in even layers. Bake for 25 minutes, stirring everything around halfway through baking time, making sure to bring the edges into the middle and vice versa. At the end of baking time, the mixture will have browned but may still feel a little soft – don't worry, as it will crisp up as it cools.

Leave to cool on the trays completely, then stir through the dried cranberries. Store in an airtight container. The granola keeps well at room temperature for 1–2 weeks, or in the freezer for up to 3 months. It also makes an awesome gift.

Makes about 750 g (1 lb 11 oz/6 cups)

**TIP**
This is absolutely the perfect thing to package up in a nice jar or cellophane bag and hand out to friends and family during the holidays. Do your hip pocket a favour and save up all your empty jam/olive/pesto jars throughout the year, so you don't have to spend a bomb on buying new ones!

# MARZIPAN, CHERRY AND PISTACHIO STOLLEN

SINCE MANY OF OUR MODERN CHRISTMAS TRADITIONS COME FROM GERMANY VIA QUEEN VICTORIA IN THE 1800s, IT SEEMS ONLY FAIR TO INCLUDE A TRADITIONAL GERMAN CHRISTMAS LOAF IN THIS CHAPTER. OK, THE REAL REASON IS THAT IT'S COMPLETELY DELICIOUS – ESPECIALLY THIS CHERRY AND PISTACHIO VERSION. BUT ISN'T IT INTERESTING THAT CHRISTMAS TREES BECAME POPULAR BECAUSE OF QUEEN VICTORIA'S GERMAN HERITAGE AND GERMAN HUSBAND? I JUST WANT YOU TO FEEL LIKE YOU'RE GETTING YOUR MONEY'S WORTH ON THE CHRISTMAS FACTS HERE.

```
110 G (4 OZ/¾ CUP) DRIED CHERRIES
60 ML (2 FL OZ/¼ CUP) BRANDY
25 G (1 OZ) BUTTER
125 ML (4 FL OZ/½ CUP) MILK
375 G (13 OZ/2½ CUPS) STRONG FLOUR
2 TEASPOONS DRY ACTIVE YEAST
55 G (2 OZ/¼ CUP) CASTER (SUPERFINE) SUGAR
PINCH OF SALT
1 EGG
½ TEASPOON GROUND CINNAMON
½ TEASPOON GROUND CARDAMOM
2 TEASPOONS VANILLA BEAN PASTE
150 G (5½ OZ/1 CUP) RAW, UNSALTED PISTACHIO NUTS
150 G (5½ OZ) MARZIPAN


TO DECORATE
25 G (1 OZ) BUTTER, MELTED
ICING (CONFECTIONERS') SUGAR
```

Put the cherries and brandy in a small saucepan over medium heat. Bring to the boil then cook for about 30 seconds. Remove the pan from the heat and set aside.

Melt the butter in a small saucepan over low heat, then turn off the heat and add the milk. Cool.

Put the flour, yeast, sugar, salt, egg, spices and vanilla in the bowl of a stand mixer fitted with the dough hook. Add the cool butter and milk and work the mixture on low speed, until everything comes together. Knead for about 7–8 minutes, or until the dough is shiny and elastic. Cover the bowl with plastic wrap and set aside to rise until doubled in size, 1–2 hours.

Line a baking tray with baking paper and preheat the oven to 180°C (350°F).

When the dough has risen, add the cherries and any liquid left in the pan, along with the pistachio nuts. Work the cherries and pistachio nuts into the dough using a dough scraper or your hands. Turn the dough out onto a floured work surface (don't worry if you lose a few add-ins) and pat into a 28 cm (11 in) oval.

Shape the marzipan into a log, just smaller than the width of your dough oval, then place it off-centre on the dough. Fold one-third of the dough over to cover the marzipan, then fold the other side over the top. Place on the lined tray, cover loosely with plastic wrap and leave to rise again for an hour. Bake the stollen for 20–30 minutes or until golden brown and hollow when tapped. Brush the still-warm loaf with the melted butter, dust liberally with icing sugar (and I mean liberally), then leave to cool completely before dusting generously again and slicing.

Makes 1 loaf

# CHOCOLATE-HAZELNUT RUGELACH

*A LITTLE CRESCENT MOON OF TENDER PASTRY, SWIRLED WITH CHOCOLATE AND HAZELNUTS – THIS IS MY FAVOURITE HOLIDAY COOKIE. RUGELACH ARE JEWISH IN ORIGIN, AND CAN BE FILLED WITH PRETTY MUCH ANYTHING, FROM JAM, NUTS AND CINNAMON SUGAR, TO CHOCOLATE AND POPPY SEEDS. BECAUSE I AM CONSTANTLY LOOKING FOR MORE WAYS TO BRING CHOCOLATE INTO MY LIFE, I FILL MINE WITH CHOCOLATE, HAZELNUTS AND A SLICK OF CHOCOLATE-HAZELNUT SPREAD. THE REAL GENIUS HERE IS THE CREAM CHEESE DOUGH, WHICH IS INDESTRUCTIBLE AND SO EASY TO WORK WITH. THE RICHNESS AND TENDERNESS OF THE PASTRY IS WHAT MAKES THESE COOKIES.*

2 TABLESPOONS CHOCOLATE-HAZELNUT SPREAD
2 TABLESPOONS CASTER (SUPERFINE) SUGAR
PINCH OF GROUND CINNAMON
75 G (2¾ OZ/½ CUP) CHOPPED MILK CHOCOLATE (60% COCOA SOLIDS)
70 G (2½ OZ/½ CUP) HAZELNUTS, CHOPPED

*DOUGH*
150 G (5½ OZ/1 CUP) PLAIN (ALL-PURPOSE) FLOUR
PINCH OF SALT
100 G (3½ OZ) BUTTER, COLD
150 G (5½ OZ) CREAM CHEESE, COLD

To make the dough, put all the ingredients in the bowl of a stand mixer fitted with the paddle attachment. Work the mixture on medium speed until the dough looks crumbly, with some larger pieces. It's ready when you can pick up the crumbly dough, squeeze it and it easily comes together in a ball.

Turn the dough out onto a lightly floured work surface and press and squeeze it together. Roll it into a short, fat log, wrap in plastic wrap and chill for at least an hour or overnight in the refrigerator.

When you're ready to bake the cookies, take half the dough and put the other half back in the refrigerator.

Tear off two pieces of baking paper and put the piece of dough between them. Roll it out into a 23 cm (9 in) circle. Spread 1 tablespoon of the chocolate–hazelnut spread over the dough.

Stir together the sugar, cinnamon, chocolate and nuts and scatter half of this mixture over the piece of dough.

Slice the dough like a pizza, into 12 wedges. Roll each wedge up from the outside in, so it looks like a little croissant.

Put the cookies on a baking tray lined with baking paper. Repeat with the next piece of dough, putting them on a second lined baking tray. Put the cookies on their trays in the refrigerator to chill for about 15 minutes.

Preheat the oven to 180°C (350°F).

Bake the cookies for 15–20 minutes, or until golden brown. Transfer to a wire rack to cool completely, before storing in an airtight container. These will keep for at least 3 days.

*Makes 24 cookies*

I HATED MINCE PIES WITH A PASSION UNTIL ABOUT 3 YEARS AGO. THEY JUST CREEPED ME OUT — WHY IS THE PASTRY SO WEIRD AND GREASY? HOW CAN THEY BE STORED AT ROOM TEMPERATURE FOR SO LONG WITHOUT GOING MOULDY? WHY IS THERE MINCE IN THE NAME? MY PROBLEM WAS THAT I WAS EATING STORE-BOUGHT MINCE PIES WHICH, TO THIS DAY, I STILL DESPISE. BUT THE HOMEMADE MINCE PIE IS A DIFFERENT STORY. BUTTERY PASTRY, FRUITY, BOOZY-RICH FILLING, AND A SHORT WINDOW IN WHICH TO EAT THEM ARE THE HALLMARKS OF A GOOD MINCE PIE. THERE'S ONLY ONE WAY TO IMPROVE THEM: STUFF THEM WITH ICE CREAM.

*FILLING*
100 G (3½ OZ/1 CUP) FROZEN CRANBERRIES
50 G (1¾ OZ) BUTTER
60 ML (2 FL OZ/¼ CUP) PEDRO XIMINEZ SHERRY
1 VANILLA BEAN, SPLIT LENGTHWAYS AND SEEDS SCRAPED
115 G (4 OZ/½ CUP, FIRMLY PACKED) BROWN SUGAR
150 G (5½ OZ/1 CUP) MIXED DRIED FRUIT
110 G (4 OZ/½ CUP) DRIED PITTED PRUNES, CHOPPED
1 TEASPOON GROUND CINNAMON

*PASTRY*
300 G (10½ OZ/2 CUPS) PLAIN (ALL-PURPOSE) FLOUR
60 G (2 OZ/½ CUP) ICING (CONFECTIONERS') SUGAR
PINCH OF SALT
115 G (4 OZ) BUTTER, COLD
1 EGG

*TO SERVE*
ICE CREAM (VANILLA OR EGGNOG FLAVOUR WOULD BE GOOD)

For the filling, put all the ingredients in a large saucepan over medium–low heat and bring to the boil. Cook for a few minutes, stirring regularly, until the cranberries are cooked through and easily smushed against the side of the pan. Smush up some of the cranberries, then turn off the heat and set aside to cool completely. Alternatively, leave to cool in the refrigerator overnight.

For the pastry, put the flour, icing sugar and salt in a food processor and blitz to get rid of any lumps. Cut the butter into cubes, add it to the flour mixture and pulse until the mixture looks like breadcrumbs. Finally, add the egg and pulse until the mixture starts to clump together. Turn the mixture out onto a piece of plastic wrap, press it into a disc, wrap it up and refrigerate for at least 30 minutes or overnight.

Preheat the oven to 180°C (350°F) and line two baking trays with baking paper.

On a lightly floured work surface, roll the dough out to about 5 mm (¼ in) thick. Cut out 24 rounds of pastry using a 7 cm (2¾ in) cutter. Put half the rounds on the lined baking trays. Put just under a tablespoon of filling onto each round. Cut a small star out of half the remaining rounds and stick on top of the others. Use the rounds to top the pies and then bake for 15–20 minutes or until golden brown and cooked through. Leave to cool completely on the trays. To serve, flip one of the pies over and wedge on a generous scoop of ice cream. Top with another pie, right-way up, and press them gently together to make an ice cream sandwich.

Makes 12 pies (6 ice cream sandwiches)

*THE COMBINATION OF GINGER AND CHOCOLATE IS SO CHRISTMASSY TO ME. I THINK IT'S BECAUSE THERE IS ALWAYS A BOX OF CHOCOLATE-COATED GINGER FLOATING AROUND SOMEWHERE AT THIS TIME OF YEAR – USUALLY AROUND MY DAD, BECAUSE HE LOVES IT. THE IDEA FOR A WATER-BASED GANACHE IS SOMETHING I PICKED UP FROM PAUL A. YOUNG, A LONDON CHOCOLATIER, IN HIS BOOK, ADVENTURES WITH CHOCOLATE. IT SAVES THIS DESSERT FROM BEING OVER-THE-TOP RICH, WHICH CHOCOLATE POTS CAN BE; YET THEY REMAIN BEAUTIFULLY SILKY, FULL-BODIED AND ELEGANT. THESE ARE ACTUALLY THE PERFECT TWO-BITE DESSERT FOR THE END OF A BIG PARTY, AND YOU WOULD GET ABOUT 8 SERVES IF YOU MADE THEM IN LITTLE SHOT GLASSES OR DEMITASSE CUPS (THE RECIPE IS EASY TO DOUBLE OR EVEN TRIPLE). OTHERWISE, YOU CAN SERVE THEM IN SMALL GLASSES OR RAMEKINS AND GET ABOUT 4–6 GREEDY SERVINGS OUT OF THIS.*

100 G (3½ OZ) MILK CHOCOLATE (60% COCOA SOLIDS)
100 G (3½ OZ) DARK CHOCOLATE (70% COCOA SOLIDS)
3 PIECES STEM GINGER IN SYRUP, PLUS 1 TABLESPOON OF THE SYRUP
125 ML (4 FL OZ/½ CUP) THICKENED (WHIPPING) CREAM (35% FAT)
2 EGG YOLKS

Chop the chocolate into small chunks and put it in a small heat-proof mixing bowl.

Chop the stem ginger into very small pieces and distribute evenly between your serving dishes or glasses.

Put the cream, reserved ginger syrup and 80 ml (2½ fl oz/⅓ cup) water in a small saucepan over medium–low heat and stir together. Heat just until small bubbles begin to form at the edges, then pour over the chopped chocolate. Leave for about 30 seconds, then begin to stir, very gently, from the centre of the bowl, until the chocolate melts and the mixture comes together. Drop in the egg yolks and stir until they're incorporated.

Divide the mixture evenly between your serving dishes or glasses and chill for at least 4 hours or, preferably, overnight.

Serves 4–6

## SALTED CARAMEL AND GINGERBREAD PUDDINGS

*IF IT'S CHRISTMAS, THEN THERE HAS TO BE GINGERBREAD. BUT I'M AN AUSSIE GIRL AND, AS MUCH AS I CANNOT LET GO OF THE IDEA THAT CHRISTMAS SHOULD BE COLD, THE SUMMER COMES AND PROVES ME WRONG EVERY YEAR. SO THIS IS MY WAY OF GETTING A GINGERBREAD FIX WITHOUT THE CRACKLING LOG FIRE AND WARM MUGS OF SPICED COFFEE. I MAKE CUTE LITTLE INDIVIDUAL TRIFLES WITH SALTED CARAMEL PUDDING!!! SORRY TO SHOUT, BUT YOU CANNOT IMAGINE HOW DELICIOUS THESE ARE. YOU'RE GOING TO WANT TO GO SWIMMING IN THEM, THEY'RE SO GOOD.*

```
1 SMALL LOAF STORE-BOUGHT GINGERBREAD (AKA GINGER CAKE)
250 ML (8½ FL OZ/1 CUP) MILK
2 TABLESPOONS CORNFLOUR (CORNSTARCH)
2 EGG YOLKS
125 ML (4 FL OZ/½ CUP) THICKENED (WHIPPING) CREAM (35% FAT)
1 BATCH SALTED CARAMEL (PAGE 9)
WHIPPED CREAM, TO SERVE
```

First, cut the gingerbread into small cubes and distribute between four small serving glasses. Reserve some crumbs for garnish.

Put 60 ml (2 fl oz/¼ cup) of the milk in a small bowl. Add the cornflour and whisk to combine, then whisk in the egg yolks.

Put the remaining milk and the cream in a small saucepan and heat over medium heat until it is steaming.

Slowly whisk the hot milk mixture into the egg yolk mixture, then pour the mixture back into the same saucepan and cook over medium heat, whisking constantly until the mixture just boils. Remove the pan from the heat.

Whisk in 190 ml (6½ fl oz/¾ cup) of the salted caramel, then pour this mixture over the gingerbread in the serving glasses.

Chill completely in the refrigerator for about 3 hours, then serve with a dollop of whipped cream, an extra drizzle of salted caramel and a sprinkling of gingerbread crumbs.

Serves 4

# SWEET CHERRY GALETTES

IN AUSTRALIA, CHRISTMAS IS CHERRY SEASON. I AM ABSOLUTELY CRAZY FOR CHERRIES AND THEY ARE ONE OF THE FEW FOODS THAT I WILL EAT MYSELF SICK ON (THE OTHERS BEING WATERMELON AND DOUGHNUTS). THIS IS THE PERFECT WAY TO TAKE FULL ADVANTAGE OF THAT BEAUTIFUL FRUIT, AND IT'S SUCH A GREAT DESSERT FOR ANY TIME YOU HAVE FRIENDS AND FAMILY OVER. THE GOOD NEWS IS THAT THESE GALETTES WORK WELL WITH FROZEN FRUIT TOO, WHICH MEANS THAT YOU NOT ONLY GET TO ENJOY THEM WHENEVER YOU LIKE, YOU ALSO GET TO SKIP ALL THAT CHERRY PITTING. BONUS!

1 EGG, BEATEN
RAW (DEMERARA) SUGAR FOR SPRINKLING

*PASTRY*
450 G (1 LB/3 CUPS) PLAIN (ALL-PURPOSE) FLOUR
PINCH OF SALT
2 TABLESPOONS CASTER (SUPERFINE) SUGAR
225 G (8 OZ) BUTTER, COLD, CUT INTO CUBES
170 ML (5½ FL OZ/⅔ CUP) ICED WATER

*FILLING*
600 G (1 LB 5 OZ/3 CUPS) PITTED CHERRIES
JUICE OF ½ LEMON
80 G (2¾ OZ/⅓ CUP) CASTER (SUPERFINE) SUGAR
1 TEASPOON VANILLA BEAN PASTE
1 TABLESPOON CORNFLOUR (CORNSTARCH)

To make the pastry, put all the ingredients, except the water, in a large bowl (or food processor or stand mixer). Rub the butter into the flour until most of the flour looks like breadcrumbs, with some larger flakes of butter throughout (or pulse a few times in your food processor, or mix on a low speed with the paddle attachment of your stand mixer, to achieve the same result). Slowly add the water while continuously stirring the mixture, just until it looks like it's about to come together – you may not need all the water. Using your hands, shape the dough into a disc, wrap it in plastic wrap and put it in the refrigerator to chill for at least 30 minutes.

To make the filling, halve the cherries and put them in a large bowl with the remaining ingredients. Toss everything together and set aside. Don't let it sit for too long, though, otherwise the moisture will draw out of the cherries and produce too much liquid.

Preheat the oven to 180°C (350°F) and line two baking trays with baking paper.

Take the dough from the refrigerator and roll it out on a well-floured surface to about 5 mm (¼ in) thick. Using a 14 cm (5½ in) plate as a guide, cut out as many rounds of dough as you can, then re-roll the scraps and cut again. You're aiming to get 8 rounds of dough.

Put the dough rounds on the lined baking trays and divide the filling evenly between them, leaving a thick border around the edge of each round. Fold the edges up and over the cherries, creating a rumpled, pleated border around the edge of each one, but leaving the cherries in the centre exposed. Brush the edges of the pastry with the beaten egg, sprinkle with raw sugar and bake for 15–20 minutes or until golden and bubbling.

Makes 8

# EGGNOG BREAD PUDDING WITH CINNAMON CARAMEL SAUCE

*EGGNOG ISN'T REALLY A PART OF MY FAMILY'S CHRISTMAS. IT'S USUALLY AT LEAST 30°C (86°F) OUTSIDE (AS ANY AUSSIE CAN ATTEST) AND A CUP OF COLD, LIQUIDY CUSTARD IS FAIRLY UNAPPEALING TO ME. BUT BREAD PUDDING, OR BREAD AND BUTTER PUDDING, IS DEFINITELY A FAMILY RECIPE THAT I EMBRACE. MY GRANDAD ERNIE USED TO MAKE IT ALL THE TIME, AND HE WOULD EVEN DO A DRIED-FRUIT-FREE VERSION FOR PICKY EATERS. HE WAS ONE OF MY FAVOURITE PEOPLE AND, IN THE SPIRIT OF HIS GENEROSITY AND EXUBERANCE, HERE IS MY CHRISTMAS VERSION OF HIS RECIPE. SERVE WITH WHIPPED CREAM OR ICE CREAM.*

### BREAD PUDDING
60 G (2 OZ/½ CUP) SULTANAS (GOLDEN RAISINS)
60 ML (2 FL OZ/¼ CUP) BRANDY
1 SMALL LOAF BRIOCHE (ABOUT 200 G/7 OZ)
5 EGGS
115 G (4 OZ/½ CUP) CASTER (SUPERFINE) SUGAR
250 ML (8½ FL OZ/1 CUP) THICKENED (WHIPPING) CREAM (35% FAT)
375 ML (12½ FL OZ/1½ CUPS) MILK
½ TEASPOON FRESHLY GRATED NUTMEG
1 TEASPOON VANILLA BEAN PASTE
30 G (1 OZ/¼ CUP) CHOPPED PECANS (OPTIONAL)

### CINNAMON CARAMEL SAUCE
230 G (8 OZ/1 CUP) CASTER (SUPERFINE) SUGAR
190 ML (6½ FL OZ/¾ CUP) THICKENED (WHIPPING) CREAM (35% FAT)
1 TEASPOON GROUND CINNAMON

Put the sultanas and brandy in a small saucepan over medium heat and bring to the boil. Turn off the heat and set aside to steep.

Slice the brioche thickly and place in a large shallow baking dish.

In a bowl, whisk together the eggs and sugar, then stir in the cream, milk, nutmeg and vanilla. Pour the custard over the brioche, scatter over the soaked sultanas and cover with plastic wrap. Set aside to soak for at least 15 minutes (or a couple of hours if you put it in the refrigerator).

Preheat the oven to 180°C (350°F).

Scatter the pecans, if using, over the pudding and bake for about 25 minutes, or until set with a slight wobble in the middle. Leave to cool while you make the sauce.

For the cinnamon caramel sauce, put the sugar and 60 ml (2 fl oz/¼ cup) water in a saucepan over high heat and cook gently, without stirring, until the sugar dissolves. Continue to cook the sugar until it reaches a dark amber colour, about 5–8 minutes, then remove the pan from the heat and carefully add the cream. Wait until it bubbles down, then add the cinnamon. Return the pan to the heat and cook until everything comes together, about 30 seconds. Set aside to cool slightly.

Cut squares of the warm pudding and serve with the cinnamon caramel sauce drizzled over and a little whipped cream or ice cream.

Serves 6–8

# CHOCOLATE AND HAZELNUT CHRISTMAS PUDDING

FOR ME, IT'S JUST NOT CHRISTMAS UNTIL I'VE BOILED SOMETHING IN A PUDDING BASIN FOR FAR LONGER THAN MAKES ANY SENSE, TURNED IT OUT ONTO A CAKE STAND AND STUCK AN ARTIFICIAL SPRIG OF HOLLY INTO THE TOP OF IT. IT HAS TO BE DONE – BUT IT DOESN'T HAVE TO BE THE SAME GLUEY, BORING PUDDING AS YOU MIGHT BE USED TO. THIS ONE DOESN'T EVEN HAVE FRUIT – BUT IT'S JUST AS CELEBRATORY AND, DARE I SAY, EVEN MORE DELICIOUS THAN THE CLASSIC PLUM PUDDING. IT'S A GIANT, MOIST, CHOCOLATEY, HAZELNUTTY DOME OF CHRISTMAS. I LOVE THIS WITH OLD-SCHOOL CUSTARD.

115 G (4 OZ) BUTTER
230 G (8 OZ/1 CUP) CASTER (SUPERFINE) SUGAR
4 EGGS
200 G (7 OZ) FINELY CHOPPED OR GRATED DARK CHOCOLATE (70% COCOA SOLIDS)
75 G (2¾ OZ/½ CUP) PLAIN (ALL-PURPOSE) FLOUR
1½ TEASPOONS BAKING POWDER
160 G (5½ OZ/2 CUPS) FRESH BREADCRUMBS (BRIOCHE CRUMBS ARE ESPECIALLY GOOD)
110 G (4 OZ/1 CUP) HAZELNUT MEAL
ICING (CONFECTIONERS') SUGAR FOR DUSTING

Butter a 1.5 litre (51 fl oz/6 cup) capacity pudding basin and line the base with baking paper.

In a bowl, cream together the butter and sugar until pale and fluffy. Beat in the eggs, one at a time, scraping down the bowl every so often. Once the eggs are incorporated and the mixture is light and fluffy, add the remaining ingredients, except the icing sugar, and stir until everything is incorporated.

Scrape the mixture into the pudding basin and cover with a layer of baking paper, then a layer of foil. Put in a large pan and add boiling water to reach halfway up the side of the pudding basin, being careful not to splash any into the pudding. Place the lid on and cook over low heat and keep on a slow boil for 2½ hours, checking the pan often to make sure it hasn't boiled dry – top up with hot water as necessary.

When the time is up, carefully remove the pudding from the water, then turn it out onto a serving plate. Dust with icing sugar and serve.

Serves 6–8

# PEPPERMINT ARCTIC ROLL

*DURING THE HOLIDAYS, THE KEY TO MAINTAINING ONE'S SANITY IS TO KNOW WHEN TO TAKE A SHORTCUT. AND I FEEL LIKE THIS PEPPERMINT ARCTIC ROLL IS THE PERFECT EXAMPLE OF THAT. THERE ARE THREE COMPONENTS HERE – THE CAKE, THE ICE CREAM AND THE SAUCE. I PROPOSE THAT YOU MAKE THE CAKE AND THE SAUCE, BUT GO AHEAD AND BUY THE ICE CREAM. THERE ARE SO MANY GOOD-QUALITY BRANDS AVAILABLE, IT'S HARD TO GO WRONG. AND, ONCE YOU'VE ROLLED THE ICE CREAM IN HOMEMADE CAKE, SMOTHERED IT IN CHOCOLATE SAUCE AND SCATTERED IT WITH CANDY CANES, WHO WILL KNOW, OR CARE?*

*CAKE*
3 EGGS
115 G (4 OZ/$\frac{1}{2}$ CUP) CASTER (SUPERFINE) SUGAR
75 G (2$\frac{3}{4}$ OZ/$\frac{1}{2}$ CUP) PLAIN (ALL-PURPOSE) FLOUR
2 TABLESPOONS UNSWEETENED (DUTCH) COCOA POWDER
500 ML (17 FL OZ/2 CUPS) MINT ICE CREAM
CRUSHED CANDY CANES, TO DECORATE

*SAUCE*
125 ML (4 FL OZ/$\frac{1}{2}$ CUP) POURING (SINGLE/LIGHT) CREAM (35% FAT)
2 TABLESPOONS LIQUID GLUCOSE (OR CORN SYRUP)
150 G (5$\frac{1}{2}$ OZ) DARK CHOCOLATE (70% COCOA SOLIDS)

Preheat the oven to 180°C (350°F) and line a 26 x 40 cm (10¼ x 16 in) rimmed baking tray with baking paper.

For the cake, put the eggs and sugar in a large bowl (or the bowl of a stand mixer fitted with the whisk attachment), and beat vigorously (or on high speed) until the mixture is tripled in volume and very pale. Sift in the flour and cocoa powder and fold gently, until incorporated.

Scrape the mixture onto the baking tray and spread out gently in an even layer – try not to mess with it too much – you don't want to lose all that air! Bake for 12–15 minutes, or until dry and it springs back when touched lightly.

Lay another sheet of baking paper on another tray and flip the cake upside down onto it. Peel off the baking paper from the underside (now the top) of the cake, and tightly roll the cake up inside the fresh sheet of paper, Swiss (jelly) roll-style. Set the rolled-up cake aside to cool completely.

When the cake is completely cool, get your ice cream out of the freezer and let it sit for 5–10 minutes to soften slightly.

Unroll the cake and spread the ice cream over it, leaving a thick border at the far edge. Re-roll the cake, wrapping it in the paper, and quickly get it into the freezer to set. Leave it in the freezer for at least 4 hours.

When you're ready to serve, make the sauce by melting the cream, glucose and chocolate together in a small saucepan over low heat.

Put the arctic roll on a serving dish, pour over some of the sauce and scatter with crushed candy canes. Serve with extra sauce on the side.

Serves 6

**TIP** If you can't find a good-quality mint ice cream, you can always add about 1 teaspoon of good-quality peppermint essence to vanilla ice cream. Or, of course, switch up the flavours to whatever you like! The pretzel ice cream on page 90 would be particularly amazing.

# CHOCOLATE TIRAMISU

*I KNOW THIS ISN'T A TRADITIONALLY CHRISTMASSY RECIPE, BUT IT'S MY BOYFRIEND'S FAVOURITE THING, SO I MAKE IT PRETTY MUCH EVERY YEAR. AND, OK, I HAPPEN TO LOVE IT TOO. THE SECRET JOY OF THIS RECIPE IS THE RIBBONS OF CHOCOLATE BETWEEN THE LAYERS. AT THE EDGES, THE CHOCOLATE FIRMS UP TO FORM LITTLE CRISPY BITS, AND IN THE CENTRE IT MELTS WITH THE COOKIES AND CREAM TO FORM A GANACHE-LIKE TEXTURE. PLUS, IT JUST LOOKS SO MAJESTIC – ALL THOSE GORGEOUS LAYERS AND SNOWY PEAKS … CAN SOMEONE PLEASE PASS ME A SPOON?*

2 LARGE EGGS
115 G (4 OZ/½ CUP) CASTER (SUPERFINE) SUGAR
500 G (1 LB 2 OZ) MASCARPONE
125 ML (4 FL OZ/½ CUP) THICKENED (WHIPPING) CREAM (35% FAT)
150 G (5½ OZ) DARK CHOCOLATE (70% COCOA SOLIDS)
1 TABLESPOON COCONUT OIL
500 ML (17 FL OZ/2 CUPS) STRONG BREWED COFFEE
A SWIG OF BOOZE – RUM, MARSALA, FRANGELICO OR BRANDY ARE ALL
  GREAT (OPTIONAL)
300 G (10½ OZ) SAVOIARDI BISCUITS (SPONGE FINGERS/LADY FINGERS)
UNSWEETENED (DUTCH) COCOA POWDER, TO DUST

Separate the eggs and put the yolks in a large mixing bowl with the sugar. Whisk together until very pale. Add the mascarpone and cream and stir together until incorporated.

In a separate bowl, whisk the egg whites to stiff peaks.

Melt the chocolate and coconut oil together in a heat-safe bowl in the microwave, in 20-second bursts on High (100%), stirring well after each burst.

Stir together the coffee and booze, if using, in a shallow bowl. Begin dipping half the savoiardi biscuits into the coffee and placing them in one layer in the bottom of a large serving dish. Drizzle over half the chocolate mixture, spreading to create a thin layer.

Fold the egg whites into the mascarpone mixture, then pour half of this over the chocolate.

Repeat the layers using the remaining savoiardi biscuits, coffee, chocolate and mascarpone until the dish is full. Dust the top layer generously with cocoa powder and then put in the refrigerator to set for at least 6 hours or overnight.

Serves 6–8

# CRANBERRY EPIPHANY CAKE

*To cap off the year in style, or to show January that I'm not going to bow to its healthy-eating dictates, I like to bake this Cranberry Epiphany cake. It's a French cake, also known as a galette des rois, made up of almond cream inside a puff pastry shell. I add cranberries because I love their sharpness and, when they're around, I like to eat them as much as possible. But almost any fruit would work just as well, or you can leave it plain and traditional.*

100 G (3½ OZ/1 CUP) ALMOND MEAL
1 TABLESPOON PLAIN (ALL-PURPOSE) FLOUR
115 G (4 OZ/½ CUP) CASTER (SUPERFINE) SUGAR
100 G (3½ OZ) BUTTER, AT ROOM TEMPERATURE
1 TEASPOON VANILLA BEAN PASTE
2 EGGS
2 SHEETS PRE-ROLLED, ALL-BUTTER PUFF PASTRY
70 G (2½ OZ) FRESH OR FROZEN CRANBERRIES
ICING (CONFECTIONERS') SUGAR TO DUST

Preheat the oven to 180°C (350°F) and line a baking tray with baking paper.

Put the almond meal, flour, sugar, butter, vanilla and one of the eggs in a large mixing bowl (or the bowl of a stand mixer with the paddle attachment). Beat vigorously (or on high speed) until everything comes together in a light, fluffy paste.

Put the 2 sheets of pastry on a work surface and cut a 23 cm (9 in) circle out of each.

Put one of the circles on the baking tray and dollop the almond mixture onto it. Spread the mixture out, leaving a 2.5 cm (1 in) border around the edge, then scatter over the cranberries.

Beat the remaining egg in a small bowl with a splash of water. Use a pastry brush to paint the border of the pastry with this mixture, making sure that none spills over the side. Top with the remaining round of pastry, pressing gently around the edge to seal. Lightly score the top with a criss-cross pattern to decorate. Brush the whole thing with the egg, then bake for 30–40 minutes or until deep golden brown and puffed. Dust with icing sugar and serve warm.

Serves 6–8

These are the songs I listened to while putting this book together, and I think they pair particularly well with all these recipes! I thought you might like 'em.

# PLAYLIST

DOLLY PARTON
**'9 TO 5'**

HUMBLE PIE
**'BLACK COFFEE'**

ARCTIC MONKEYS
**'THE BAKERY'**
(ACOUSTIC VERSION)

THE ROLLING STONES
**'BROWN SUGAR'**

RED HOT CHILI PEPPERS
**'CAN'T STOP'**

EAGLES
**'VICTIM OF LOVE'**

THE LONELY ISLAND
**'HUGS'**

THE STROKES
**'YOU ONLY LIVE ONCE'**

DAVID BOWIE
**'MOONAGE DAYDREAM'**

JIMMY FALLON,
CROSBY, STILLS & NASH
**'FANCY'** (COVER)

LITTLE BIRDY
**'DO RIGHT WOMAN'**
(COVER)

SHE & HIM
**'SLEIGH RIDE'** (COVER)

SHE & HIM
**'BABY IT'S COLD OUTSIDE'**
(COVER)

## ACKNOWLEDGEMENTS

Firstly, thank you to Seane Parsonson, the Kurt to my Goldie, the Garth to my Wayne, the Tango to my Cash. I love being your girl on the side and I couldn't have done ANY of this without you. Any of it, like, at all. So from the bottom of my heart, I love you, I like you and thank you. Big time.

Thank you Mum and Dad, Suzanne and Michael, for giving me your encouragement and support even when I was quitting my job, dropping out of university and attempting to make money from a food blog. I couldn't ask for better cornermen.

Thanks to Paul McNally for giving me this opportunity, and being so super-chill and easy to work with. Thank you to Rachel Day for all your hard work and commitment in bringing this whole project together, and to Mark Campbell for dealing with my strong design opinions diplomatically, and making sure I looked presentable in the photos.

Many thanks to Miss Vicki Valsamis, for being a badass food stylist, having amazing taste in music, and painting my nails about three times a day on the shoot. Thank you Chris Middleton for taking all these beautiful photos, and being patient with my incessant photography questions. Thank you to Aileen Lord for being such a generous host, a ridiculously creative and talented designer, and such a positive and encouraging person to be around. Ariana Klepac, thank you for making the editing process absolutely painless – a feat I didn't think was possible.

Thanks to the friendly, relaxed and talented Caroline Jones for making sure that the food actually got out of the kitchen, and to Jemima Good for your totally indispensable help and for not flinching when I started throwing fake karate moves at you.

## ABOUT THE AUTHOR

SARAH COATES IS THE WRITER, PHOTOGRAPHER, STYLIST AND RECIPE DEVELOPER BEHIND THE SUGAR HIT! A PANCAKE AFICIONADO FROM WAY BACK, SARAH'S LOVE OF FOOD BEGAN THE MINUTE SHE HIT THE HIGHCHAIR. SHE WAS AN UNUSUAL CHILD IN THAT THERE WAS NO SMEARING OF FOOD OVER HER FACE, THE WALLS OR THE CHAIR – SHE MADE SURE THAT FOOD WENT IN HER MOUTH! FAST FORWARD TWENTY YEARS AND SARAH STILL SPENDS MOST OF HER TIME THINKING ABOUT HER NEXT MEAL. SHE SPENDS THE REST OF HER TIME CREATING AND PHOTOGRAPHING EPIC RECIPES TO SHARE WITH FAMILY, FRIENDS AND HER COMMUNITY OF REGULAR BLOG READERS. THE SUGAR HIT! IS AN AWARD-WINNING RESOURCE FOR AND COMMUNITY OF LIKE-MINDED LOVERS OF KICK-ASS FOOD.

FIND THE SUGAR HIT AT THESUGARHIT.COM

Published in 2015 by Hardie Grant Books
Hardie Grant Books (Australia)
Ground Floor, Building 1
658 Church Street
Richmond, Victoria 3121
www.hardiegrant.com.au

Hardie Grant Books (UK)
5th & 6th Floors
52–54 Southwark Street
London SE1 1UN
www.hardiegrant.co.uk

A Cataloguing-in-Publication entry is available from the catalogue of the
National Library of Australia at www.nla.gov.au
The Sugar Hit!
ISBN 978 1 74379 040 3

Publishing Director: Paul McNally
Project Editor: Rachel Day
Editor: Ariana Klepac
Design Manager: Mark Campbell
Designer: Aileen Lord
Photographer: Chris Middleton
Stylist: Vicki Valsamis
Home Economist: Caroline Jones
Home Economist's Assistant: Jemima Good
Production Manager: Todd Rechner

Colour reproduction by Splitting Image Colour Studio
Printed in China by 1010 Printing International Limited

Tim Tam is a registered trademark of Arnott's.

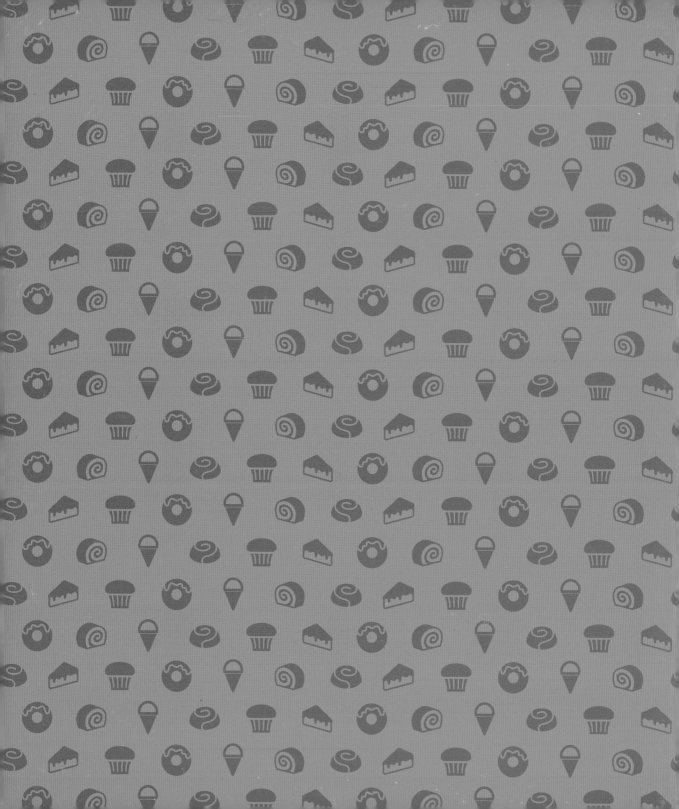